floyd's fjord fiesta

ALSO BY KEITH FLOYD

Floyd on Fish

Floyd on Fire

Floyd on France

Floyd on Britain and Ireland

Floyd in the Soup

Floyd's American Pie

A Feast of Floyd

Floyd on Oz

Floyd on Spain

Floyd on Hangovers

Far Flung Floyd

Floyd on Italy

The Best of Floyd

Floyd on Africa

KEITH FLOYD

floyd's fjord fiesta

MICHAEL JOSEPH · LONDON

MICHAEL JOSEPH

Published by the Penguin Group

Penguin Books Ltd, 27 Wrights Lane,
London W8 5TZ, England

Penguin Putnam Inc., 375 Hudson Street,
New York, New York 10014, USA

Penguin Books Australia Ltd, Ringwood,
Victoria, Australia

Penguin Books Canada Ltd, 10 Alcorn Avenue,
Toronto, Ontario, Canada M4V 3B2

Penguin Books (NZ) Ltd, 182-190 Wairau Road,
Auckland 10, New Zealand

Penguin Books Ltd, Registered Offices:
Harmondsworth, Middlesex, England

First published 1998

1 2 3 4 5 6 7 8 9 10

Set in Bodoni and Frutiger

Printed in England by
Butler & Tanner Ltd, Frome and London

A CIP catalogue record of this book is available
from the British Library

ISBN 0–718–14303–5

contents

WINTER

Norway 10

Sweden 68

SUMMER

Norway 84

Denmark 128

Sweden 150

Greenland 190

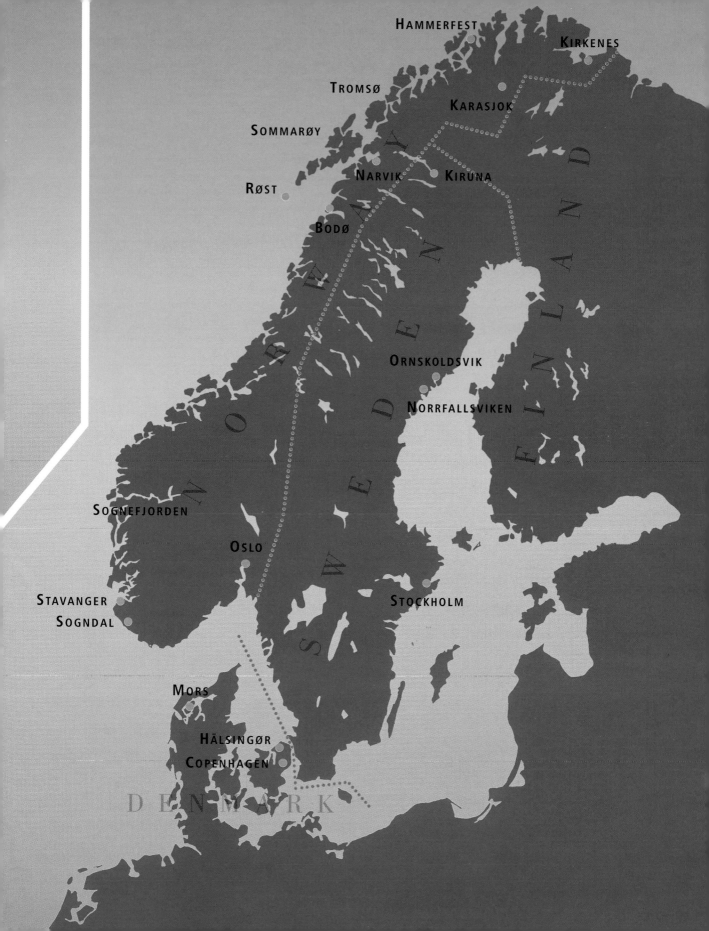

WINTER

norway

We had been waiting three weeks for our luggage to arrive in Malaga from Dublin until, just twenty-four hours before we set off for the frozen north, it became clear that it would not arrive in time. All our carefully packed moonboots, balaclavas, survival suits, gloves and thermal underwear were still sitting in a transit warehouse in Tangiers and would not arrive until after our departure.

Our first destinations were so remote that there was no possibility of buying what we needed there, so my wife and I, in T-shirts and shorts, drove frantically to the largest department store on the Costa del Sol to re-equip ourselves.

At first the bemused store manager thought we were barking mad requesting, on this hot, sunny Mediterranean day, thermal underwear, ski suits, gloves, scarves and the like, but after a lot of rummaging around in basements we managed to obtain more or less what we needed and, thus equipped, we boarded a plane for the first leg of our journey on Air Iberia, whose in-flight food at least is a cut above that of many other airlines, to London Heathrow and overnighted in an appalling airport hotel. Even I, a very seasoned traveller, having spent the last few months eating crunchy tuna salads, fresh anchovies, exquisitely roasted milk-fed lamb washed down with inexpensive and highly drinkable Spanish wines, was shocked into a sudden loss of appetite by the poor quality of food that such places present at vast expense to their captive travelling customers. So we spent the night in the bar drinking and eating plain white-bread ham sandwiches and watching in dumb horror as ill-trained bar staff failed to operate an espresso machine or prepare an Irish coffee.

O, to be in airport England now that spring is here!

And so we set off for a frustrating day of four flights and lost luggage from London to Oslo, Oslo to Bodø, Bodø to Leknes and Leknes to Røst, a barren collection of tiny, flat, treeless, grassless islands north-west of Norway and just in the Arctic Circle. The flight from Bodø via Leknes took us over spectacular snowscapes of jagged mountains and glittering, silver fjords, through brilliant blue skies with a huge, red sun hovering sleeplessly on the horizon.

The Dash 8 made a smooth landing on Røst's tiny airstrip and we disembarked into the prefabricated shed that served as the airport terminal. Our 'roadie', Adrian Worsley, was waiting with a taxi to take us and our luggage into 'town'. But, of course, there was no luggage. To lose the lot on its way from Ireland was something we had come to terms with but, after our frantic efforts in Marbella, to lose a second lot was downright irritating!

Our first impressions of Røst were of a desolate, eerie tranquillity at odds with a screaming Arctic wind that blows without interruption or hindrance from hills, mountains or forests. Flat landscape is covered in simple pine-log A-frames, making silver-grey tunnels sometimes several hundred metres long, with thousands and thousands of pairs of cod hanging to dry in the inhospitable wind.

The taxi-driver sped recklessly along the narrow road to the main harbour, past a scattering of very pretty prefabricated wooden houses, cheerfully painted in soft pastel yellows, blues, reds and purples. The harbour, with its piers and wharfs built on wooden stanchions, is dominated by the cod-processing factory. Small wooden barrels of cod roe were stacked high, waiting to be shipped out and sent around the world. The cod-liver-oil processing plant stood idle now that the main season of cod fishing had ended. Dozens of brightly painted and varnished fishing boats were bobbing in the evening sunlight as the smooth sea rolled in. It was eleven o'clock at night and brighter than an English midsummer day.

Left: Do sheep have cold legs?

Right: Røst, flat, bleak and desolate, but the vibrant fishing community offers ornithologists and killer-whale watchers a welcome more comforting than a hot toddy and a plate of toasted crumpets taken before a log fire

Overleaf: The view from my bedroom window: magnificent

There was no hotel on the island, so the management and crew were quartered in the Seaman's Mission. This was a sort of youth hostel with a heavy religious atmosphere – hymn-books and Bibles scattered on Formica canteen tables, a large picture of Jesus as a shepherd, crook in hand, knocking on a cottage door (or should that be knocking on Heaven's door?), 'No Smoking' signs and a total ban on alcohol. We fared rather better, as one of the two shopkeepers on the island had lent us a basic but very warm apartment looking over the harbour and out to the only feature for miles, the steeply rising Puffin Island, where huge sea eagles glided, disdainfully ignoring the aggressive black-backed gulls in the incredible light of the Norwegian night.

As in all remote communities, the locals were hospitable and helpful, and we were quickly lent some clean, warm clothes. Then we were officially welcomed to the island by the mayor and the community at a party in a wooden fish loft, which was incredibly cold; cheering, slightly haunting accordion music accompanied a meal of salt-cod fritters and salad, followed by boiled dried cod and boiled potatoes with a dessert of cloudberry syllabub, everything washed down with bottles and bottles of aquavit. At about two o'clock, exhausted by travelling, numbed by the cold and intoxicated by the aquavit, we stumbled to the warmth of our triple-glazed apartment.

By this time our wayward luggage had arrived, strapped into the passenger seat of a 1953 biplane heroically piloted by a character we nicknamed 'Biggles'. Despite our tiredness of the day before, we slept badly because of the unfamiliarly bright night, but were in good spirits now that we had met our Norwegian film crew, who were clearly a good bunch. We failed to catch the name of the cameraman, so we nicknamed him 'Vlad the Impaler'. There were also Bernt, the sound man, Odd, quickly renamed 'Odd Bod', lighting and second camera, Pal, the producer, Stein, the boss, and Merte, the production assistant. In addition, of course, there were the English rabble: Mike Connor, the director, Stan the Man, my manager, Scott Rattray, my assistant, the aforementioned Adrian, Kim Sayer, stills photographer, and, of course, me.

The calm before the storm: the infamous Puffin Island in the background.

You will have to read on to discover why ...

Left: The hostile climate of Røst creates perfect conditions for drying cod, which hang by their hundreds of thousands before being packed and exported all over the world

Right: Home is the fisherman, home from the sea ... but I bet there's no honey for tea

We joined everyone for breakfast at the Seaman's Mission before shooting the first cooking sketch on this Arctic mini-break.

I arrived at the location, where Scott had laid out a table groaning with cod. Huge whole fresh cod, hard dried cod, salted cod, cod tongues, cod liver and cod roe. Basically a lot of cod was on show on the edge of beautifully bleak tunnels of hanging dry cod, swinging in the screaming wind; even a stoutly secured canvas windbreak could not stop the Calor gas rings from blowing out every two or three minutes. (To the curious locals who had assembled, along with a couple of Norwegian television crews, journalists and radio stations, the bright sunshine, a light wind and a temperature of only minus five betokened a spring day.)

Our last great adventure had been under the burning sun in Africa, and there I was faced with the problem of all our foodstuffs and crew melting under relentless sun and heat. Here, by the time I had assembled the dish, everything was frozen solid and, with the stove burning only intermittently, sauces would freeze before I could finish cooking them. However, where there's a will there's a way, as they say, and I somehow managed to poach some exquisitely fresh cod with a creamy parsley sauce enriched with chopped cod liver, whipped up some taramasalata from a huge smoked roe and sautéed cod tongues (they resemble scallops a little) with olive oil, onions, garlic and fresh tomato sauce, much to the amazement of the onlookers. The standard approach to their basic diet of cod, or for that matter lamb or puffin, is to boil it and serve it with boiled potatoes.

FLOYD'S REAL TARAMASALATA

Serves 4 or more

450g (1lb) smoked cod's roe

4-6 garlic cloves, crushed

1 tablespoon fresh white breadcrumbs

juice of 2-3 lemons

150ml (¼ pint) extra virgin olive oil

salt and ground white pepper

Put the cod's roe, garlic and breadcrumbs into a food processor or blender and whizz together until smooth. Add the lemon juice, and then slowly dribble in the olive oil, with the motor running, until you have a smooth, creamy spread. Add a bit of salt and white pepper, if you need to. Serve with fresh bread.

POACHED COD WITH FRESH PARSLEY SAUCE

Serves 4

600ml (1 pint) milk

1 carrot

1 celery stick

1 onion, halved

a few parsley stalks

1 bay leaf

half a dozen black peppercorns

4 x 225g (8oz) cod fillets

40g (1½oz) butter

40g (1½oz) plain flour

225g (8oz) cooked cod liver – see below, or leave out

1 large bunch of parsley, chopped

150ml (¼ pint) double cream

salt

Put the milk, carrot, celery, onion, parsley stalks, bay leaf and peppercorns into a large frying-pan, big enough to take the fish fillets. Bring to the boil, reduce the heat and simmer for a few minutes. Add the cod fillets and poach gently for 5-6 minutes until the fish is cooked (the flesh should flake easily and look opaque).

Lift the fish from the pan and keep it in a warm place. Strain the fish cooking liquid, discard the vegetables, herbs and what-have-you (these were just used for their flavour) and let it cool down a bit. In a saucepan, melt the butter and stir in the flour. Cook gently for a minute or so and then gradually add the fish cooking liquid. Heat, stirring all the time, to make a smooth sauce.

Now if you're using cod liver, cook it for a few minutes in butter, and then chop it and stir it into the sauce (otherwise just leave it out). Add the parsley and cream, and reheat gently, being careful not to let it boil; season with a shake of salt. Serve with the fish, accompanied by a big dish of buttered new potatoes.

We returned to the Seaman's Mission, and after a basic lunch of fried chicken and chips, interviews and non-alcoholic beer, we prepared for the afternoon cooking sketch, which was to be filmed aboard an eighteen-foot fishing boat anchored off Puffin Island a couple of kilometres away. At the same time, we would put out hand-lines and catch some cod, which when caught, filmed and edited, would, by the magic of television, appear to be the very same cod that I had prepared earlier. Also, because killer whales had been sighted in the area, Mike Connor, the director, decreed that the killer whales should appear at around seven in the evening, as they would make splendid visual images of the Arctic. He had also ordained that Puffin Island would be festooned with thousands of puffins, and that, no matter which way the tide or the wind took the boat, it should lie in photogenic sympathy with the sun, the island and the soaring eagles. Directors, you see, operate with an authority that can only be achieved by the Great Dictator in Heaven! Also, for some strange reason, directors do not know how to use walkie-talkies, and do not employ the services of translators. With a cavalier disregard for the problems that would occur with fishermen who already thought us quite mad and who spoke no English, Mike shouted out his directions in vain and unheard over the chugging of noisy diesel engines and the screaming wind, clutching his head in despair as he watched three boats, two of which should have been steaming in parallel and one of which should have been bringing up the rear, roar off at full speed in completely opposite directions. And yet, despite the absurdity and the impracticability of Mike's requirements, after a couple of hours of total confusion, we had achieved the cooking sketch, filmed the killer whales and caught some fish. Well, actually one fish, and that turned out to be a haddock, not a cod.

Four things you don't need when trying to do a sophisticated cooking sketch: a tiny fishing boat, a choppy sea, an Arctic wind, a Norwegian TV news crew and a fisherman who thinks you're barking mad and um ... puffins ... OK, I know that's six, but I could have gone on

These little islands and the surrounding cruel seas are of huge interest to ornithologists and naturalists. The area is a magnificent haven of rare sea birds and killer whales, who, when on a feeding frenzy, leap majestically out of the ocean, their white bellies flashing in the sun – and here lies the nub. Let me explain.

For centuries, the seven hundred or so souls of Røst have existed on a basic diet of cod, boiled mutton and boiled puffin, and although today they are a prosperous community, they still occasionally like to eat the odd puffin, and in this the mayor of Røst is at loggerheads with the mainland administration and current popular thinking, which is that puffins are a protected species and should not be hunted. Now, even if 50 per cent of the population of Røst ate a puffin once a week, which I can assure you they absolutely do not do, there is no way that they could significantly deplete the population of puffins, which arrive in Røst annually in their millions. I have to say, I take the mayor's point of view. Certainly if, during the Second World War, the islanders of Røst had not so generously donated their natural resources, many people in occupied Europe and elsewhere would have starved. Be that as it may, this is only meant to be a light-hearted journal of my travels, so we won't dwell on the rights and wrongs. But I had no idea of the furore I would create by pan-frying a couple of breasts of imported puffin and serving them with a berry sauce with sour cream and beetroot chips while freezing my goolies off on the deck of an unstable fishing boat. For your information, the recipe does not appear in this book, but puffins taste a lot like teal, much admired by gourmets and hunters alike throughout Europe.

The last word on the puffin saga must go to the skipper of our little fishing boat, who confided through our Norwegian translator that puffins couldn't taste right cooked in the few minutes I had taken. His wife, who had been cooking them for years, had always boiled them for at least three hours and served them with boiled potatoes.

The next morning, due to the lack of blackout curtains, we were awake at four in the morning, and since breakfast was not until six, we spent a couple of hours working on recipes and notes for this book. From the window of the apartment, we could see a storm gathering far beyond Puffin Island, and within a few minutes the island was obscured by a roaring blizzard. The blizzard passed and the sun twinkled on the now snow-covered slopes of the island. The weather seemed to change every ten minutes, alternating between scudding clouds, bright sunshine and blizzards; the one constant factor, however, was the bitterly cold wind, which blew relentlessly.

Our location that morning was a quaint little farm only yards from the ocean. On the horizon, massive white mountains soared dramatically into the perfect blue sky. The dish was to be a version of the island's delicious salt-grazed boiled lamb. In the past, the Lofoten Islands, to which Røst belongs, was about the only part of Norway that could sustain sheep farming, which continues there to this day.

We had rounded up some sheep as extras in order to set the scene. They were munching sheep nuts in a tiny stone-walled, snow-covered paddock. Behind the wall, the sea was crashing violently over the flat grey

Sheep have been reared on Røst and the surrounding islands since time immemorial, even before climatic changes made it possible on the mainland. They graze on saltmarshes and taste delicious

Same sheep and mad
Englishman are out in the
midnight sun

shore. The sky was immense, and I, struggling against the wind, was preparing a turmeric, anchovy, caper and dill sauce. I was halfway through, when, from nowhere, we were obliterated by a raging blizzard. The sheep had finished their nuts and, bored, had wandered out of frame. The wiry farmer started to coax them back with his bag of fodder, but Adrian and Stan the Man were both under the impression that, if you shouted loud enough and waved your arms about, Norwegian sheep would perform like highly trained actors. A sort of 'Wild North' show erupted. Directors' syndrome seems to be catching.

Of course, the sheep stampeded and there was fifteen minutes of complete chaos before calm was restored and shooting continued. The locals, who had gathered to watch and knew how to deal with stampeding sheep, looked on encouragingly, enjoying the impromptu cabaret. By this time, my delicate creamy sauce had frozen solid and the local farm dog had run off with the leg of lamb, which I had placed on the ground in the snow to stop it from cooking any further. It worked: it never got cooked any further!

We had no time to spend another three hours poaching the replacement lamb, so we boiled it furiously for twenty minutes to give it the appearance of being cooked and shamelessly resorted to the talents of my wife, who was once a food stylist. The situation was saved and we trooped wearily back, frozen to the marrow, for some fried chicken and chips (again) at the mission.

Braised Leg of Lamb with Turmeric, Capers, Anchovy and Red Peppers

The locals told me that they would normally boil a leg of lamb in water, flavoured with an onion, and would then make a white sauce with the stock, flavoured with chopped fresh dill. Delicious and simple, I am sure, but I felt that their excellent salt marsh lamb deserved tweaking up a bit.

Serves 4-6

1 leg of lamb, weighing about 2kg (4½lb)

6 carrots, peeled and cut into thick batons

2 onions, peeled and studded with
    a dozen cloves

3 leeks, white part only, sliced

6 celery sticks, cut into batons

3 bay leaves

a few dill or parsley stalks

1 tablespoon salt

Sauce

25g (1oz) butter

25g (1oz) plain flour

2 red peppers, deseeded and diced

1 tablespoon ground turmeric

50g (2oz) capers, rinsed and drained

50g (2oz) anchovy fillets, rinsed and chopped

300ml (½ pint) double cream

freshly ground black pepper

4 eggs, hard-boiled (we used seagull's eggs)

fresh dill or parsley, to garnish

To braise the lamb, put it into a very large cooking pot, cover it with cold water and bring to the boil. Reduce the heat, skim off any scum and then add all the vegetables, herbs and salt. Cover and simmer for about 3 hours, after which time the meat will be really tender. Strain off 600ml (1 pint) of the stock, reserving the vegetables.

Now for the sauce. Melt the butter in a saucepan, add the flour to make a roux and then cook over a low heat for a minute or two. Gradually add the strained lamb stock and bring the mixture to the boil, stirring all the time.

Add the red peppers and turmeric to the sauce and cook for a couple of minutes, chuck in the capers and anchovies and pour in the cream. Heat gently without boiling, check the seasoning (it's unlikely that you'll need any salt) and then pour over the carved lamb. Serve with the vegetables from the pot and garnish with hard-boiled eggs and fronds of dill or parsley.

The Norwegian papers arrived with massive coverage of our presence on the island, all of it positive and friendly except for one banner headline of 'Floyd Cooks Endangered Species'. The hapless journalist was still hanging around and got very short shrift indeed when he bounded up to our table to ask how we had liked the piece. Unluckily for him, at that precise moment the London papers started to phone, so he was unceremoniously – because it was he who had informed them – ejected, which was a pity, as he was in fact the mayor's son. The mayor had been very good to us, so it was all very unfortunate. There was a nagging feeling in the crew that we had been set up for somebody's political end.

After lunch, we boarded some fishing boats and spent a freezing five hours filming GVs (general views), shots of the harbour, shots of the hills, shots of the boats, shots of me arriving in the harbour, shots of me leaving the harbour and so forth. All this to the total bewilderment of our extremely helpful skippers, who could not understand why filming always takes place backwards, or why they had to do the same manoeuvre again and again. For that matter, sometimes, neither do I.

After the GVs we spent a couple of hours doing walking GVs and by half past nine, for the first time in several days, we were relaxing with a few drinks in front of the television which hung from the bar of the island's only pub, Stephanie's, which the owner had opened specially for us. Here, to our great amusement, we watched ourselves on the nine o'clock news. Once again our salty old dog of a skipper had the final word. 'They have no sense of time,' he said, 'and I don't think they know anything about boats.' From his point of view, of course, this was an astute and accurate comment, but thanks to the help given us by him and his colleagues, we had got some dramatically beautiful shots.

We left Røst in the middle of a searing blizzard in the ubiquitous Dash 8, which was obliged to discard some passengers in favour of our luggage and filming equipment, much to their distress. Eight hours later, after three take-offs and three touchdowns, we finally arrived in Tromsø, which was three

It's great to go travelling, but
even better to get home

metres deep in snow. The hotel room, with magnificent views of the harbour and the snowy peaks in the distance, was luxurious compared to our last few days in Røst. But our delight turned to dismay when we discovered that alcohol is not served on Sundays. So, being resourceful folk, we sat in a quiet corner of the hotel, furtively sipping whisky from our own supplies, only to be discovered by the hotel manager, who berated us thoroughly for committing this cardinal sin.

We breakfasted early in order to take yet another flight still further north and driving to Karasjok, in Finmark, home of the Lapland people and millions of reindeer. Over breakfast we were entertained by two drunk Russian

This is the most exhilarating way to travel during the mush hour; no road rage here

fishermen, who had evidently fallen out after an all-night drinking session, and were punching the living beJesus out of each other on the snow-covered jetty outside our window. Karasjok boasted a warm, welcoming wooden hotel with a self-service launderette, a well-stocked bar and reindeer steaks on the menu. It was so cold we were all issued with Arctic survival suits. So, walking like Michelin men, we sped around the bleak but beautiful snowscape on roaring, high-speed snow scooters or swished eerily through the snow on creaking wooden dog sledges. We bored holes into the ice of frozen lakes and fished for char, we herded reindeer and prepared exquisite dishes, which within

This young Sami girl will travel hundreds of kilometres with her family and their herd of reindeer to seek the summer coastal pastures

minutes of being put on the plate were frozen solid – you could snap off a piece of lettuce or a sprig of dill, but you certainly couldn't eat it. Another problem, of course, was trying to get hold of ingredients. Here, high up in the North Cape, nothing much grows, the few shops only stock basic foods and most people are happy to eat reindeer: boiled reindeer, fried reindeer, stewed reindeer, reindeer heart, smoked reindeer, dried and marinated reindeer. And if you get a bit bored with that, you could have excellent Norwegian salmon: grilled salmon, poached salmon, gravadlax, dried salmon, salmon eggs, fried salmon, raw salmon. You get my point?

It was at this stage of the journey that I realized north Norway is not exactly a gastronomic paradise, so I abandoned my original plan of cooking local dishes and instead decided to apply Mediterranean and Asian cooking techniques to Scandinavian ingredients, which was great fun and extremely liberating, because I don't think that seven half-hour television programmes of boiled reindeer would have gone down too well.

Mother's Pride takes on a
new understanding in a reindeer
tent in the frozen north

The *MV Polarlys* plys the North Cape, bringing essential supplies like food and engine parts, mail and homecoming families to the isolated communities, some of which are inaccessible by road in winter. It is also a great cruise ship

Massive King Crabs like this one have defected from Russia to find a new home in Norway, where they adorn the tables of smart Oslo restaurants. Delicious but expensive

Our sojourn in Karasjok over, we headed north yet again to the town of Kirkenes, not far from the Russian border, where, under the sinister shadow of an abandoned military lookout border tower, I trudged on snowshoes, falling headlong into two metres of soft snow from time to time, to an absurd location – a trench dug in the snow overlooking Russia – and cooked some bear, a meat which is highly thought of in these parts and very expensive to boot. I am afraid to say that Kirkenes in winter is an ugly, depressing little town, and we were therefore delighted to embark on a luxurious coastal express, the *MV Polarlys*, which shuttled between Kirkenes and Bergen, a journey which takes eleven days, stopping at every community along the coast, delivering essential supplies to the remote, and except by sea, inaccessible villages. In its magnificent galley I cooked fine fillets of halibut with a red pepper sauce.

HALIBUT WITH RED PEPPER SAUCE AND BEETROOT CRISPS

Virtually every day on this trip, I had beetroot with my breakfast. I love beetroot. So, for the officers and captain of the *MV Polarlys*, I prepared this fanciful creation. They were very polite about it.

Serves 4

225g (8oz) pickled beetroot

6 tablespoons crème fraîche

1 lemon, halved

sea salt and freshly ground black pepper

4 red peppers, halved and deseeded

2 medium raw beetroot, peeled and very thinly sliced

oil for frying

3 tablespoons olive oil

1 tablespoon sun-dried tomato purée (or ordinary will do)

a dash of balsamic vinegar

700g (1½lb) potatoes, quartered

50g (2oz) butter

4 halibut fillets or steaks, weighing about 225g (8oz) each

chopped dill or chives, for garnish

Rinse and drain the pickled beetroot, and purée it in a blender or food processor with the crème fraîche and the juice from half a lemon. Season, transfer to a bowl and chill until later.

Pop the peppers, skin side uppermost, on to a grill rack. Grill until the skins begin to blacken and char. Turn off the grill, shut the grill compartment door and leave the peppers in the steamy atmosphere for about 15 minutes, after which time it will be easy to peel them, so do so. While you are waiting, deep-fry the thinly sliced beetroot in hot oil. Drain on kitchen paper and season with salt.

Now put the peeled peppers into the rinsed-out blender or food processor and whizz to a purée with 2 tablespoons of olive oil, the tomato purée and balsamic vinegar. Season and pass the mixture through a fine sieve. Put into a small pan and heat gently. Put the potatoes on to cook.

Heat some butter in a frying-pan until it starts to foam. Add the remaining tablespoon of olive oil so that the butter doesn't burn and whack in the fish fillets or steaks. Sear them for 2 minutes on each side and then squeeze over the juice from the other half of the lemon. Cook for another minute or two until the fish is cooked – the flesh must be opaque, so check with a fork.

Pour a pool of the red pepper sauce on to 4 warmed plates, top with boiled potatoes, tossed in butter, then place the fish on top and add a spoonful or two of the pink beetroot dressing. Scatter some beetroot crisps on top and garnish with dill or chives.

We disembarked at Hammerfest the following day, a pretty harbour with brightly painted houses twinkling in bright sunshine, and took the plane back to Tromsø and on to Sommarøy. There, on a warm sunny day, on a beautiful sandy beach surrounded by snow-covered mountains, we, along with the entire population, had a wonderful beach barbecue where we were confronted by something very dear to Norwegian hearts – a fishcake. This is a rather bland mixture of raw fish and potato flour, first boiled and then reheated on the barbecue. I managed to inject a bit of fun and flavour by frying them in olive oil and serving them with a sweet and sour sauce while the villagers were barbecuing catfish and cod cheeks.

Fishy frolics in the sunshine, washed down with a little moonshine

Fjord Fish Cakes with a Sweet and Sour Sauce

Serves 4

300g (10oz) cod, skinned and boned

300g (10oz) haddock, skinned and boned

100g (4oz) potato flour (or use polenta)

salt and white pepper

cold milk, to bind

vegetable oil, for frying

Sweet and sour sauce

2 tablespoons sesame or soya oil

1 bunch spring onions, sliced into 2cm (¾ inch) pieces

1 carrot, sliced into matchstick pieces

1 red pepper, deseeded and thinly sliced

3 garlic cloves, finely sliced

50g (2oz) root ginger, peeled and cut into thin slices

6 tablespoons light soy sauce

3 tablespoons dark muscovado sugar

3 tablespoons rice or light malt vinegar

2 teaspoons cornflour

coriander leaves, to garnish

First of all, make the sweet and sour sauce. Heat the sesame or soya oil in a wok or large frying-pan and add the spring onions, carrot, red pepper, garlic and ginger. Stir-fry for a couple of minutes. Mix together the soy sauce, sugar, vinegar and cornflour, and add to the vegetables, cooking for 2-3 minutes until thickened and smooth. Keep warm.

Put all the fish into a food processor with the potato flour (or polenta). Season with salt and pepper. Turn out, and if necessary mix in a little cold milk to make a workable consistency. Shape into small fishcakes, and fry them in hot oil for about 5 minutes on each side until golden brown. Drain on kitchen paper and serve with the sweet and sour sauce, garnished with fresh coriander.

Tromsø, the Paris of the North, endures some of the highest snowfalls in Norway, sometimes up to six or seven metres. But life, thank the Lord, goes on

MEDALLIONS OF WHITE FISH OR SCALLOPS

Serves 4

12 cod tongues (yes, cod do have tongues, but as lots of fish are prepared
    at ports these days, the heads are lopped off before they are sold, so
    you may have difficulty tracking them down; you can use about 700g
    (1½lb) monkfish, firm white fish or scallops instead)

50g (2oz) plain flour

salt and freshly ground black pepper

100ml (3½fl oz) olive oil

1 onion, finely chopped

3 garlic cloves, crushed

3 fresh red chillies, deseeded and finely chopped

3 fresh green chillies, deseeded and finely chopped

150ml (¼ pint) fresh tomato sauce (see page 49)

a handful of chopped fresh parsley, chervil, coriander or basil

Trim the cod tongues or cut the monkfish (or other substitute) into
medallions. Sprinkle the flour on to a plate and season with salt and pepper.
Roll the cod tongues (or substitute) in the flour.

    Heat the olive oil in a large frying-pan. Add the floured tongues (or
substitute) and brown on both sides. Then add the onion, garlic and chillies
and cook over a medium high heat for about 4 minutes. Heat the tomato
sauce. To serve, place tomato sauce on to the plate and arrange the cod
tongues, monkfish or scallops on top with the garlic, onion and chillies.
Garnish with parsley, chervil, coriander or basil.

Salt Cod with Potatoes in Tomato Sauce

Generally, salted or dried cod is simply boiled and served with potatoes, melted butter, lemon juice and dill. But I think salt cod is utterly delicious and decided to cook it in this Spanish fashion.

Serves 4

1 thick piece of salt cod, weighing about 500g (1lb 2oz) soaked in plenty
    of cold water for around 4 hours and then rinsed in fresh water

6 tablespoons olive oil

1 large onion, sliced

600ml (1 pint) fresh tomato sauce (see page 49)

2 small, hot chillies, deseeded and chopped

a few sprigs of fresh dill or parsley

freshly ground black pepper

500g (1lb 2oz) potatoes, peeled and thickly sliced

Soak the cod and rinse it, as above. Preheat the oven to 190°C/375°F/Gas 5.

Heat the olive oil in a large flameproof casserole and add the onion, cooking gently for about 15 minutes. Add the tomato sauce and chillies and cook for a few minutes more.

Cut the rinsed salt cod into chunks and add them to the cooking pot with the sprigs of dill or parsley. Give it all a good stir, season with a bit of black pepper and layer the sliced potatoes on top. Transfer to the oven and bake for about an hour, until the potatoes are tender.

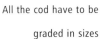

All the cod have to be

graded in sizes

FRESH TOMATO SAUCE

Makes 450ml (³/₄ pint)

3 tablespoons olive oil

1 red onion, finely chopped

3 garlic cloves, crushed

700g (1¹/₂lb) ripe tomatoes, skinned
 and chopped

1 tablespoon muscovado sugar

2 tablespoons malt vinegar

1 tablespoon chopped fresh parsley

1 tablespoon chopped fresh basil

300ml (¹/₂ pint) water

salt and freshly ground black pepper

Heat the olive oil and sauté the onion and garlic until softened but not browned. Add all the other ingredients to the pan, bring to the boil and then lower the heat. Simmer for about 30 minutes, without a lid, so that the liquid reduces and the flavour concentrates. Remember to stir the sauce from time to time. Check the seasoning, adding salt and pepper to taste.

TARTARE OF CHAR WITH ROSTI POTATO

Char, a member of the salmon and trout family, thrives in the icy lakes of Finmark. It has a fine, delicate flesh that the Norwegians like to ferment underground; whereas I decided to apply a little Japanese influence to this very fresh, raw fish.

Serves 4

2 char, or trout, salmon, mackerel, etc. (weighing about 450g/1lb each), skinned and filleted

4 tablespoons crème fraîche

100g (4oz) lumpfish roe or any caviar, such as salmon or sturgeon

Lime and ginger marinade	*Potato rosti*
finely grated zest and juice of 2 limes	3 large potatoes, quartered
150ml (¼ pint) groundnut oil	1 onion
25g (1oz) fresh root ginger, peeled and finely	100g (4oz) clarified butter
chopped	salt and freshly ground black pepper
pinch of salt	fronds of fresh dill or parsley sprigs, to garnish
pinch of sugar	
1 red chilli, deseeded and finely chopped	

To begin with, chill the fish fillets in the freezer for half an hour before slicing. In the meantime, make the marinade by mixing together the lime zest and juice, groundnut oil, ginger, salt, sugar and chopped chilli.

Slice the fish as thinly as possible into 8cm (about 3 inch) lengths. Pop the strips into the marinade, cover and leave for an hour.

Meanwhile, make the rosti. Grate the potatoes and the onion in a food processor, if possible. Mix with a couple of tablespoons of the melted clarified butter, and season well with salt and black pepper. Form into rounds about 1cm (roughly ½ inch) thick, and fry in the remaining clarified butter, for about 4–5 minutes, until golden brown on both sides.

Place the rosti in the centre of your serving plates and top with spoonfuls of crème fraîche. Arrange the fish around the outside and garnish with the caviar and fresh herbs. Spoon the remaining marinade around the fish.

Grilled Char with an Asian Sweet and Sour Stir-fry

Serves 2

2 char or trout, bream, bass, etc. (weighing about 400g/14oz each), cleaned

salt and freshly ground black pepper

6 tablespoons sesame or stir-fry oil (a seasoned oil that tastes
    exceptionally good)

1 red pepper, deseeded and sliced into thin strips

50g (2oz) fresh root ginger, peeled and finely sliced

2 garlic cloves, finely sliced

1 small cucumber, peeled, halved lengthways, deseeded and sliced
    into strips

2 red chillies, deseeded and sliced

3 spring onions, trimmed and sliced

4 tomatoes, skinned, deseeded and sliced into strips

3 slices of pineapple (fresh is best), cut into chunks

a good splash of rice wine or dry sherry

soy sauce, to taste

bunch of fresh chives

Brush the fish on both sides with some of the oil, and season with salt and black pepper. Cook on the barbecue over hot coals, or grill them until the flesh is opaque – about 3 minutes on each side.

While they are cooking, stir-fry the vegetables. Heat the rest of the oil in a wok or large frying-pan. Add the red pepper and stir-fry it for 1 minute, then add the ginger and garlic. Stir it around the wok for a few seconds, and tip in the cucumber, chillies and spring onions. Stir-fry for a couple of minutes, and add the tomatoes, pineapple and rice wine or dry sherry. Stir-fry for a moment or two more. Add the chives just before serving.

Put the fish on to warm serving plates and tip half the vegetables over each portion. Season with a good splash of soy sauce and serve.

KARASJOK REINDEER HEART

In the UK, and no doubt in America too, heart is hardly ever served, which is a pity because it is inexpensive, nutritious, fat free and full of flavour.

Serves 4

2 reindeer hearts (or 4 lambs' hearts)

50g (2oz) bacon fat

25g (1oz) butter

1 onion, finely chopped

225g (8oz) button mushrooms, quartered

100ml (3½fl oz) Swedish aquavit (or use brandy or cognac)

a large wineglass of crowberry wine (or use madeira or port)

300ml (½ pint) decent stock

a handful of chopped fresh parsley

freshly ground black pepper

pinch of saffron strands

Quarter the hearts, and remove all the sinew and fat with a pair of scissors. Season with a little salt. Heat a frying-pan and add the bacon fat, sizzling it to render down the fat. Add the butter and then the heart, cooking briskly to seal the meat on both sides.

Chuck the onion and mushrooms into the pan, and cook until the onion begins to brown; add the aquavit (or brandy or cognac) and flame it with a match. Let the flames die down, and then remove the heart, onion and mushrooms from the pan using a slotted spoon; keep in a warm place.

Add the wine (or madeira or port) to the pan and bubble it until the liquid has reduced by half. Add the stock, bring to the boil and cook for a couple of minutes. Return the heart, onion and mushrooms to the pan and add the parsley. Heat through, season, and serve with rice which you have flavoured and coloured with a generous pinch of saffron strands.

SAUTÉ OF REINDEER WITH PAPRIKA

Serves 4-6

3 tablespoons olive oil

1kg (2¼lb) rump of reindeer (failing that, venison, beef or veal),
    cut into chunks

4 onions, chopped

2 garlic cloves, crushed

225g (8oz) smoked streaky bacon

1 or 2 glasses of aquavit (or cognac or brandy)

6 tomatoes, skinned and chopped

1 tablespoon of tomato purée

3 tablespoons mild paprika

500ml (16fl oz) beef stock

12 juniper berries, lightly crushed

2 star anise

salt and freshly ground black pepper

150ml (¼ pint) fresh soured cream

fresh dill or chives, to garnish

In a very large, heavy-based saucepan, heat the olive oil; then add the reindeer meat (or venison, beef or veal) a handful at a time, allowing each handful to sear and brown before adding the next. This is important – it gives the dish its flavour. Next add the onions, garlic and bacon, cooking over quite a high heat for about another 5 minutes, stirring often.

Now add the aquavit, cognac or brandy and set light to it with a match – or just let it bubble excitedly for a few minutes to drive off the alcohol. Next add the tomatoes, tomato purée and paprika, stirring well. Pour in the stock and add the juniper berries and star anise. Bring up to the boil and then reduce the heat to a gentle simmer. Cover and cook slowly for 1½ hours, or thereabouts, until the meat is tender and the sauce is thick with little tears of olive oil floating on the rich, red sauce. Check the seasoning, adding some salt and pepper as needed.

Serve the dish, topped with a dollop of soured cream and fronds of fresh dill or snipped fresh chives. Don't forget to fish out the star anise – they can be a bit chewy.

GRATIN OF KING CRAB AND LETTUCE PARCELS

Serves 4

1 large live king crab

Court bouillon

2 litres (3¼ pints) water

1 carrot, sliced

1 celery stick, sliced

1 onion, sliced

bay leaf, thyme, peppercorns and parsley stalks

half bottle dry white wine

1 teaspoon salt

For the parcels

3 Cos or romaine lettuce (or spinach, or Chinese leaves)

salt and freshly ground black pepper

40g (1½oz) butter, plus a good knob for greasing

40g (1½oz) plain flour

150ml (¼ pint) double cream

100g (4oz) Jarlsberg or Cheddar cheese, grated

1 tablespoon chopped mixed fresh herbs (tarragon, chives,
    parsley and chervil)

First of all, you need to cook the crab (or get someone else to do it for you). Failing that, buy a ready-cooked crab, but make sure you inquire about when it was cooked – it needs to be fresh. If you are doing it, put all the ingredients for the court bouillon into a large saucepan with a tight-fitting lid and bring to the boil. Plunge in the crab, slam on the lid and cook for 15 minutes. Lift out the crab and allow it to cool for a while. Don't throw out the cooking liquid.

Sit down at the kitchen table with an array of instruments to break the crab and remove the meat – a mallet or rolling-pin, kitchen scissors, teaspoon and skewers, and a couple of bowls – one for the meat, the other for the bits to be discarded. Extract all the meat, first from the claws, then from the body cavity, winkling it all out with the skewer. The inedible bits are the lungs and gills (or dead man's fingers) and the stomach sac. You might also need to chuck out any red rubbery bits, which are the beginnings of a new shell.

Put all the shell pieces back into the crab's cooking liquid. Heat and simmer for 20 minutes without a lid to reduce it a bit. Strain this liquid through a fine sieve and reserve it.

Now to make the parcels. You need lots of large lettuce leaves (save the others for a salad). Put them into a large colander and pour boiling water over them to wilt them. Lay them out on a work surface, divide the crab between them, season and roll up into tight, neat parcels. Line them up in a buttered gratin dish.

Next melt the butter in a saucepan, add the flour and mix to make a roux. Cook gently for a minute; then remove from the heat and gradually add 450ml (¾ pint) of the reserved liquid. Bring to the boil, stirring non-stop, until

thickened. Remove from the heat, add the cream and check the seasoning. Pour over the lettuce parcels and scatter the cheese on top. Transfer to a very hot oven (220°C/425°F/Gas 7) for about 10-15 minutes so that the cheese is bubbling and golden – or place under a hot grill for the same effect. Sprinkle with the herbs and grind over more black pepper. Serve with julienne of leeks, deep fried in hot oil.

Take four large crab claws ...

BEAR WITH LINGONBERRIES ON A CELERIAC ROSTI

Serves 4

700g (1½lb) bear loin (or beef, venison or marinated leg of pork)

3 tablespoons olive oil

a knob of butter

salt and freshly ground black pepper

a good splash of brandy or aquavit

200ml (⅓ pint) crème de cassis

300ml (½ pint) good beef stock

1 tablespoon redcurrant compote (fresh redcurrants simmered with
     sugar until syrupy) or redcurrant jelly

100g (4oz) lingonberries (or elderberries, redcurrants or blackcurrants)

Celeriac rosti

1 large potato, peeled and coarsely grated

half a celeriac, peeled and coarsely grated

75g (3oz) butter

1 tablespoon olive oil

salt and freshly ground black pepper

Slice the bear (or beef, venison or pork) into thin escalopes. Heat the oil and butter in a frying-pan and fry the meat over a high heat. Season with salt, add the brandy or aquavit and set light to it. Allow the flames to subside, then add the crème de cassis. Lift the meat from the pan and keep warm.

Add the stock to the pan, whisking with the pan juices, and then add the redcurrant compote or jelly and the berries. Season to taste with salt and plenty of black pepper – the sauce needs to be quite spicy.

To make the rosti, rinse the potato and celeriac in a colander, mixing them together. Drain well and pat dry with a clean tea towel or kitchen paper. Melt half the butter and mix in, seasoning with salt and pepper, then shape into little mounds and fry in the remaining butter and the olive oil for about 12 minutes or so, turning over once, until golden brown and crunchy. Serve with the bear and pour the sauce around.

I don't think

Tesco stocks it ...

... but here on the

Russian border it is

highly prized

BORTSCH

Bortsch is not a soup widely served in Scandinavia. I was prompted to cook it during my sojourn in Kirkenes where many of the signs were in Norwegian and Russian, and road signs pointed to such places as Murmansk.

Serves 6

1 whole Aylesbury duckling

1kg (2¼lb) raw whole beetroot, trimmed and scrubbed, but not peeled

3 litres (5 pints) chicken stock or water

2 carrots, peeled and left whole

1 onion, studded with cloves

1 leek, trimmed and halved

2 bay leaves

a few juniper berries

a couple of star anise

salt and freshly ground black pepper

fresh soured cream, to serve

fresh chives, to garnish

Put the duckling into a very large cooking pot with the beetroot, stock or water, carrots, onion, leek, bay leaves, juniper berries and star anise. Season with some salt and pepper.

Bring the whole lot to the boil, reduce the heat, partially cover and simmer gently. After about 40 minutes, lift the beetroot from the pan. Let them cool down a little and then peel them. Carry on cooking the duck for another hour. In the meantime, slice the beetroot into matchstick strips.

When the duck is cooked, lift it from the pan and allow it to cool for a few minutes; then strip off the meat, remove the skin and cut it into thick slices, complete with the skin. Strain the cooking liquid, discarding all the vegetables, and return it to the pan. The liquid will be rather fatty, so let it settle and then skim off the fat.

Return the beetroot and sliced duck to the pot, reheat it thoroughly and check the seasoning. Ladle into soup bowls and garnish each portion with soured cream and some fresh chives.

FRESH FRUITS WITH AN AQUAVIT-GLAZED SABAYON

Serves 6

4 egg yolks

75g (3oz) caster sugar

half a glass of dry white wine

3 tablespoons aquavit

selection of fresh fruits – strawberries, redcurrants, orange segments,
    blueberries, bananas, raspberries, passion fruit, or anything else
    that you like

300ml (½ pint) double cream

1 tablespoon caster sugar

Place a large heatproof bowl (metal, if you have one) over a pan of simmering water. Add the egg yolks, sugar, wine and aquavit, and beat with a balloon or spiral whisk until the mixture is really thick, frothy and glossy – this will take about 5 minutes. Let the mixture cool for just a few moments while you arrange the fresh fruits on ovenproof plates or in shallow bowls.

Whip the cream in a chilled bowl until it holds its shape and then fold it into the frothy sabayon sauce. Pour it over the fruits, sprinkle with a little caster sugar and whack the desserts under a very hot grill to brown the surface. Eat at once.

CRAYFISH BISQUE

Serves 6 or so

2kg (4½lb) freshwater crayfish, crab, lobster or saltwater crayfish

3 litres (5 pints) fish stock or water

150ml (¼ pint) olive oil

100g (4oz) butter

2 celery sticks, finely chopped

1 bulb of garlic, the cloves separated, peeled and chopped

3 carrots, finely chopped

1 leek, chopped

1kg (2¼lb) tomatoes, skinned, deseeded and chopped

2 tablespoons tomato purée

quarter bottle of brandy

half bottle of dry white wine

4 bay leaves, a few sprigs of thyme and a few crushed peppercorns

450ml (¾ pint) single cream

chopped fresh dill

Plunge the crayfish into boiling fish stock, bring back to the boil and cook for 4 minutes. Take them out (reserving the cooking liquid), let them cool for a few minutes and then peel them, removing the black intestinal vein that runs under the centre tail section. Retain the shells and set the tail meat to one side.

Heat the oil and 25g (1oz) butter in a very large pan and add the celery, garlic, carrots and leek. Fry for a few minutes until golden and then add the tomatoes and tomato purée. Add the brandy, ignite with a match and flame for a moment or two. Then add the wine, strained fish stock, herbs and peppercorns. Bring up to simmering point and bubble for 20 minutes or so.

Meanwhile, make the crayfish butter for flavouring the bisque by tipping the crayfish shells into a food processor. Add the remaining butter and whizz together until blended. Stir into the soup and strain through a fine sieve. Return to the saucepan, stir in the cream and add the crayfish meat. Heat until almost boiling, check the seasoning and serve, garnished with some chopped dill.

sweden

After the day's filming in Sommarøy, I clambered into a 1951, two-seater Piper Cub with a wooden propeller, and headed for Narvik en route to Kiruna in Sweden where, several kilometres below ground, I cooked chicken with shiitake mushrooms in one of the world's largest iron-ore mines — it produces sixty to seventy thousand tons of iron ore per day. The mushrooms were provided by a retired mineworker who had discovered that a disused mine shaft provided the perfect environment for mushroom farming. Another cooking sketch completed, I boarded a De Havilland Beaver, fitted with snow skis, on the frozen lake outside Kiruna and flew south to Norrfallsviken, an outrageously pretty, red-roofed, timber-built community where, in front of Sweden's press and media corps, I was invited to sample the famous Swedish fermented herring known as 'strumming'; a highly esteemed national dish with such a pungent aroma that you are not allowed to eat it inside. I think it

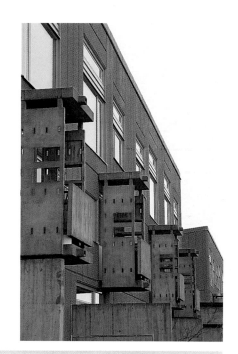

Below left: Merrily
Mining Mushrooms

Left: The A-shift
waiting to go down
the shaft

Below: The wonderful
Beaver was waiting to
take me away

Right: Miners' flats
in Kiruna

is quite the most awful thing I have ever eaten. I would rather swallow a mouthful of rotten mushrooms washed down with a glass of bleach, but manfully and heroically, even though I say it myself, I complied with the merry jape.

Good Herrings! Gosh, what a lot of fish

On a much more exciting note, however, chugging out to sea in an uncomfortable swell and a skin-freezing wind, I spent happy hours hand-hauling nets groaning with flipping, flapping, silver-flashing Swedish herrings, so firm and sweet from the icy waters. And, once again, because I realized that every Swede knows more about marinating or pickling herrings than I would ever learn, I decided to prepare them in a Mediterranean fashion. As with the freshwater fish, Sweden gave me the opportunity to cook excitingly with fine, prime ingredients.

The first phase of our journey, the winter leg, was over. Although often uncomfortable and extremely tiring, the journey was brilliant. Fabulous scenery, the thrills of seeing white Arctic hares, moose and ptarmigan, the majestic fjords, the warmth and welcome of the people we had met, the incredible serenity of a husky sledge ride, left us all overwhelmed. We had an end-of-shoot party, said our farewells and flew to Stockholm, where I was invited to sign some books in the leading bookshop. I couldn't imagine that anyone would turn up. It was pouring with rain, and I was sure that no one would have heard of me, much less have bought any of my books. To my amazement and utter delight, the bookshop was packed with public, press, radio and TV, grannies and children, cooks and architects, husbands and wives. As I signed books I was invited to taste and comment upon the great Swedish meatball, sausages with bread and mustard, and the many flavours of aquavit, all the while explaining where I had been and where I was going while grappling with the spelling of Swedish Christian names and being quizzed on my knowledge of The Stranglers band.

I had also been booked to appear for one hour on live radio to do an interview for a children's programme. I expected to twiddle my thumbs for half that time. In the event we were there for over four hours and reluctantly turned down invitations for parties, dinner, etc. for that night because the Norwegian contingent had to depart for Oslo and the Brits for London. There we were met some two hours later by a very nice man from customer services who informed us – you've guessed it – that regrettably our luggage had not been loaded on to the plane . . .

CHICKEN WITH SHIITAKE MUSHROOMS

It was a bizarre experience travelling hundreds of metres underground, into one of the world's largest iron mines, to find a retired miner growing shiitake mushrooms on birch mulch in a disused part of the mine. It was even stranger cooking these mushrooms in front of bemused miners sitting in the works' canteen, scoffing huge slabs of meatloaf at the end of their shift. Needless to say, any type of mushroom goes well with this dish.

Serves 4

4 chicken breasts, with the skin left on
salt and freshly ground black pepper
75g (3oz) butter
a large glass of brandy
a large glass of decent red wine
100g (4oz) streaky bacon, thinly sliced
100g (4oz) baby onions or shallots
240ml (8fl oz) good chicken stock
2 bay leaves
1 sprig of thyme
225g (8oz) shiitake mushrooms – or any other type that you fancy
2 garlic cloves, peeled
handful of chopped fresh parsley

Season the chicken breasts with salt and pepper. Melt a good knob of butter in a frying-pan and add the chicken breasts, cooking them for about 5 minutes on each side until golden. Add the brandy, ignite it with a match and cook for a few moments until the flames die down. Remove the chicken, add the red wine to the pan and cook for a minute or two to deglaze it.

Meanwhile, put the streaky bacon into a large flameproof casserole dish or saucepan and heat until crisp. Add the onions after a minute or two and cook until browned. Add the chicken, the chicken stock and the red-wine pan juices. Throw in the bay leaves and thyme, and bring to the boil; then reduce the heat and simmer for half an hour until the sauce is rich and syrupy.

Just before serving, melt the remaining butter in a frying-pan and sauté the mushrooms and garlic for 3-4 minutes. Chuck in some chopped parsley and season with salt and pepper. Serve with the chicken.

SMOKED HERRING WITH LEEK AND POTATO CAKES

The Swedes lightly smoke herrings not much larger than sardines. They are quite delicious, and in a smart restaurant I have no doubt that this would be described as a warm smoked herring salad and would be wrecked with a raspberry vinegar dressing.

Serves 4

25g (1oz) butter

2 leeks, trimmed and finely chopped

500g (1lb 2oz) potatoes, cooked and mashed

2 egg yolks

2-3 tablespoons double cream

salt and freshly ground black pepper

50g (2oz) plain flour

olive oil or butter, for frying

1 red apple, diced

1 medium pickled beetroot, drained and diced

225g (8oz) crème fraîche

2 tablespoons chopped fresh chives

500g (1lb 2oz) smoked herring fillets

mixed salad leaves, to serve

red onion rings and lemon wedges, to garnish

Melt the butter in a frying-pan and sauté the leeks for about 5 minutes until softened, but not browned. Mix with the mashed potatoes, egg yolks, cream and seasoning. Use your hands to shape the mixture into little patties, dust them with flour and fry in olive oil or butter (or a mixture of both) until golden and crunchy – about 4 minutes per side.

While they are cooking, mix together the apple, beetroot, crème fraîche and chives to make a salad. Season with salt and pepper.

When the potato cakes are done, serve with the herrings and beetroot salad, accompanied by the salad leaves and garnished with red onion rings and wedges of lemon. If you like, drizzle over a little extra olive oil.

FRESH HERRING FILLETS WITH A LEMON AND MUSTARD CREAM

I recall that as a child, when I lived in Wiveliscombe in Somerset, the fishmonger bought his van round every Friday. So, Friday lunch-time we always had deep-fried cod and chips, and for Saturday tea either baked, soused herrings (that is, cooked with onions and malt vinegar) or fried herrings with Granny's mustard sauce. This is my version.

Serves 4

8 herring fillets
50g (2oz) plain flour
salt and freshly ground black pepper
50g (2oz) butter
juice of 2 lemons
2 teaspoons smooth Dijon mustard
150ml (¼ pint) double cream
2 egg yolks
fresh dill, fennel or chives, to garnish

First of all, dust the herring fillets in the flour, which you have seasoned lightly with salt and pepper. Melt most of the butter in a big frying-pan, and cook the herring fillets quickly – about 4-5 minutes at the most. Remove them from the pan and keep them in a warm place.

Add the lemon juice to the frying-pan, bubbling it up to deglaze the pan juices (which makes the most of all the delicious flavours from the fish). Add the mustard and a splash of cream, whisking together till 'liaised', or smooth. Then over a low heat, whisk in the remaining butter, the egg yolks and the remaining cream, until thickened and smooth. Strain through a fine nylon sieve and serve with the herrings. Garnish with some dill, fennel or chives.

WHOLE HERRING COOKED IN A MEDITERRANEAN VINAIGRETTE

Serves 6

6 herrings
4 tablespoons olive oil
2 red peppers, deseeded and diced
1 green pepper, deseeded and diced
1 red onion, very finely sliced
a dozen or so black peppercorns
3 garlic cloves, thinly sliced
half a lemon, thinly sliced
5 tablespoons wine vinegar
6 plum tomatoes, skinned, deseeded and sliced
3-4 tablespoons chopped fresh parsley
sea salt and freshly ground black pepper

Scale, gut and rinse the herrings, leaving their heads on (ask your fishmonger to oblige). Next heat the olive oil in a large frying-pan and add the red and green peppers. Cook for a couple of minutes and then add the red onion, peppercorns, garlic and lemon.

Pour in the vinegar and bring to the boil; then add the herrings and tomatoes and cook slowly for 5 minutes. Add the chopped parsley. Turn the herrings over and simmer gently for another 5 minutes until the fish are cooked. (Test with a fork – the flesh should be opaque.)

Season with sea salt and pepper, and allow the fish to cool down in the sauce, chilling well before serving.

Fresh or delicately smoked, Swedish herrings are one of my favourite delicacies

CARBONADE OF MOOSE

Now I know you can't buy moose in Sainsbury's, but it is, after all, only another edible kind of meat and they like it in Sweden very much. To my mind, it is more like stewing veal than beef and, I have to say, jolly tasty.

Serves 8

75g (3oz) butter

about 6 tablespoons olive oil

8 large onions, thinly sliced

1kg (2¼lb) moose loin (or beef or veal)

about 75g (3oz) plain flour

200ml (⅓ pint) aquavit or gin

3 carrots, cut into long batons

2 tablespoons tomato purée

1 tablespoon juniper berries, lightly crushed

4 garlic cloves, crushed

1 teaspoon black peppercorns, crushed

2 bay leaves

1 tablespoon chopped fresh thyme

1 tablespoon chopped fresh parsley

750ml (1¼ pints) lager, stout or beer

salt

Heat the butter and 3 tablespoons of olive oil in a large frying-pan. Tip in the onions and fry them until they begin to caramelize – this will take about 20 minutes. In the meantime, cut the moose (or beef or veal) into slices, dredge them with flour and beat into thin escalopes with a meat mallet or rolling-pin. Season with salt.

Remove the onions from the frying-pan and set aside. Heat another 2-3 tablespoons of olive oil in the pan, and add the meat, searing over a high heat for a minute or two on each side. Pour in the aquavit or gin, ignite with a match, cook till the flames subside and then remove the meat from the pan.

Return the onions to the pan and add the carrots, tomato purée, juniper berries, garlic, peppercorns, bay leaves, thyme and parsley. Heat and stir together for a few moments.

If you go down to the woods today, you're sure of a big surprise

In a large flameproof casserole dish, arrange alternate layers of the meat with the onion mixture until it is all used up. Pour the lager or beer over the top, bring to the boil; cover and transfer to the oven and cook at 180°C/350°F/Gas 4 for about 2 hours, until the meat is tender. Alternatively, simmer gently on top of the hob. Serve with mashed or sautéed potatoes or pasta.

SUMMER

norway

Oslo street entertainers
are sensational

A hot Friday afternoon in July. We were sitting at a table on the pavement outside the Grand Café watching the world go by on the elegant, tree-lined boulevard that glides from the Parliament building past the university and theatre to the Royal Palace on the hill. Blue electric trams hissed past, speeding roller-bladers swooped by at terrifying speeds. In the park opposite, a troop of dazzlingly clothed Africans swayed in a trance to the hypnotic throb of drums. In a café to my right the guitarist was singing; the man eating fire while riding a unicycle was pulling more and more spectators; a couple of mandolin- and flute-wielding musicians dressed in cloaks and long baggy trousers tucked into Cossack boots were singing seventeenth-century madrigals at my whisky.

The roofs of the fine brick and stone buildings flashed with giant neon advertisements. Coach after coach pulled up at the Grand Hotel: the first disgorged serenely smiling Japanese, another, garrulous French, a third, a load of excited, open-mouthed Americans from a cruise ship that had travelled from the frozen north to this buzzing city that is Oslo.

Just past the hotel, the boulevard runs into an elegantly pedestrianized area of squares filled with bars, boutiques and restaurants. It was teeming with people, fresh-faced Scandinavians clutching bottles of beer, Japanese silently videoing. A Mayan Indian band were playing exquisitely haunting music on their flutes, maracas, guitars and drums while cocky young men bungee-jumped in reverse from a massive mobile crane, accompanied by Men at Work's 'Down Under' booming from two huge speakers. I have to say that Oslo centre is a serious threat to Dublin's Grafton Street for sheer entertainment and atmosphere.

We ambled slowly along and found ourselves in the docks. The waterside restaurants and the floating cafés were packed. Three-masted schooners gazed down at the happy throng. Ferries and hydrofoils buzzed in and buzzed out. We had a meal of excellent sushi and a sukiyaki, which was spoiled because instead of providing light beef broth, they fobbed us off with some thick, sweet Vegemite-style liquor in which to cook our thin slices of beef and fresh, crunchy vegetables. It was now midnight and the place was

This tray of drinks was
purchased and paid for by my
director, Mike Connor, at
1.25 pm on Friday, 22 July 1997.
This is the only known record
of such an act

really jointed. We were taking a drink in the still warm night and listening to the singer, when he was suddenly attacked by a fluffy-penguin-bearing young woman who, as the signs pinned to her dress clearly announced, was about to be married and was having her last drunken fling of freedom, urged on by her caterwauling mates. It was funny for two or three minutes, but after twenty, it was sad.

We took the lift to the seventh floor of our hotel and sipped cocktails with the smart set in the rooftop bar. At two the bar closed, but Oslo didn't! And, despite triple glazing, heavy blackout curtains (because of the very short nights at this time of year) and the regular curtains, the noise from the boulevard made sleep impossible. They partied till the break of day. I pulled the curtains back – on the steps of the Parliament, a couple of derelicts were helping each other across the road, clutching their bottles: two young men embraced each other passionately, kissed, waved and parted; a refuse truck ground slowly by and the trams began to run.

Another typical Oslo street entertainer at work

The Irish have poteen, the French have Eau de Vie, Germans have schnapps, the Chinese have Multoi, the Portuguese have Aqua Dienta and the Norwegians have many flavours of aquavit, the water of life

It was Saturday morning and I was to do a cooking sketch in front of a bar in the square. The street entertainers came back at midday, there was a fine six-piece a cappella group singing Bill Withers's 'Lean on Me'. A huge crowd gathered as I cooked couscous with nuts and raisins, griddled scallops on the plancha and stewed mussels in coconut milk. The audience was smiling but silent. When the dish was finished, I invited them to taste it. No one moved. They were frightened of the camera. I was standing there nonplussed, almost paralysed, when there was suddenly a spontaneous round of applause. Once the camera had gone, they devoured the food like vultures clawing at a carcass. People asked for autographs and gave us presents. My wife was given a screwdriver, a typical Norwegian joke, with a phallus as a handle. I was given home-made jam, wine and aquavit. We were inundated with invitations to drink, to eat, to party. But we were too tired to accept and opted to eat an excellent burger in the Grand Hotel café and have an early night, for the next day we were to fly to the fjords.

MUSSELS IN SAFFRON CREAM

Absolutely ignorant of what I might find in the way of ingredients in Scandinavia, before I left my home in Spain, I stocked up on a sort of emergency larder of Mediterranean aromatic spices, herbs, etc., including a very large tin of saffron that I used liberally throughout the journey. It can so subtly, but so strikingly, enhance the flavours of the simplest dish.

Serves 4

2.5 litres (4 pints) mussels

a jolly generous pinch of saffron strands

a large knob (at least 50g/2oz) butter

2 shallots or a small onion, very finely chopped

2 garlic cloves, very finely chopped

juice of 2 lemons

a handful of fresh parsley, chopped

600ml (1 pint) double cream

salt and pepper

To rid the mussels of any sand, muck and general debris, tip them into a colander and put into the sink with the cold tap running over them (slowly) for about an hour. Then arm yourself with a suitable implement – a short, sharp knife – and scrape off the barnacles and beards (the long stringy bits). Chuck out any damaged mussels or ones that remain open when tapped sharply.

Put the saffron strands into a cup and pour over about 4 tablespoons of boiling water – no need to measure it though. Leave them to soak for a while.

Take a huge saucepan that has a lid, and melt the butter. Add the shallots or onion and garlic and fry them gently for about 4-5 minutes. Now add the lemon juice, the mussels and the parsley. Put the lid on, turn up the heat for a few moments and wait for the mussels to open.

Quickly stir the saffron liquid (including the strands) into the cream and add it to the saucepan. Replace the lid and bring just to boiling point. Remove the lid and simmer for a minute or two, giving all the ingredients a gentle stir. Season with a little salt and pepper and serve, chucking out any mussels that remain shut.

On Sunday morning we breakfasted early in a high-ceilinged room with splendid chandeliers and fine views of the boulevard. Late-nineteenth-century murals celebrated Oslo's rich and famous clientele in which, of course, Ibsen, who was a regular at the Grand Hotel, features large. I am sad to say my copies of *A Doll's House* and *Peer Gynt* were lying unread in the bottom of my suitcase.

At its best, breakfast in Norway, and throughout Scandinavia, can be a very fine feast indeed. There are cheeses, hams, smoked meats and sausages; there are salmon and herrings, herrings in mustard sauce, herrings in tomato sauce, pickled herrings, herrings with onion, herrings with dill; there are eggs, soft- and hard-boiled, fruit cake, pickled beetroot, pickled cucumbers, sweet milk, sour milk, light milk, buttermilk, yoghurt, butter, margarine, wonderful varieties of bread, caviar, salmon eggs, glorious waffles with wonderful fruity jam and cream or waffles with thin slices of some unspeakable brown block cheese; there are juices, coffee, toast and tea, salads and tomatoes, rare roast beef, endless cereals and really excellent jams and preserves.

We sat on the raised section by the windows, surveying the magnificent buffet and sipping fresh juice in the sunny Sunday-morning calm. Waitresses were checking flower arrangements. Young chefs in their crisp white uniforms made their final checks of the buffet. The floor manager surveyed all from his raised lectern. A soft aroma of freshly baked bread drifted gently around the room. Seconds later the doors crashed open and 120 shrill French tourists surged through the doors and engulfed the room, circumnavigating the circular buffet. The young chefs were flattened as a wave of the most determined invaded the inner sanctum of the buffet, too impatient to wait for their compatriots to finish piling food on their plates on the correct side. They ducked, they dived, they clawed, they grabbed, they attacked the buffet like staghounds in at the death. The staff, who had clearly seen this a million times before, were totally unperturbed, and with great good humour swiftly replenished the stocks, only to be hit by the second wave of completely mystified Japanese, who came away with plates of melon and fish, bacon and jam and cornflakes with yoghurt and marmalade on top. Meanwhile, the French were back for second helpings. We watched, fascinated, as one elderly French couple each made seven separate visits to the buffet. They ate enough for ten, but after each successful raid, and with yet another handful of napkins, set about, over the next hour and a half, filling a huge shopping bag with yoghurt, butter, bread, ham, eggs, cheese, tomatoes, sausages and croissants, topped up with Grand Hotel plates, knives, forks and spoons.

Of course, with Gallic logic, not to mention Gallic avarice, they could clearly justify it to themselves on the grounds that they had paid for it, and might as well take advantage of it. Again the beleaguered and embattled staff poured from the kitchen laden down with magnificent comestibles held high above their heads (done not so much for international restaurant pizazz but rather to stop the dreaded Frognozealeans from attacking them before they reached their destination).

Brave Japanese, perhaps realizing that their initial choice of bacon and jam was not quite what they wanted, risked life and limb to return to the buffet to find something more acceptable to their taste, only to be outmanoeuvred by a phalanx of shell-suited Americans who just didn't have enough hands to carry away their booty of waffles with bacon and jam, and five or six tubs of yoghurt piled high with croissants and caviar. We saw one woman tip a jug of iced water into the sink beside the buffet and fill it with milk from the refrigerated dispenser. She returned four times to fill the jug. We decided that the plumbing had broken down in her room and she needed a bath.

Now, dear reader, if this sounds unreasonably xenophobic, it is only because my beloved manager, Stan – 'Give me the full monty' and 'I want a proper cup of tea, not this Darjeeling shit!' – was not there to redress the balance. In fact, Mrs F and my good self were the only Brits in the joint on that particular morning and, needless to say, our manners are impeccable.

So, much enriched by this close encounter of the gastronomic kind, we climbed into the reassuring womb of a Wilderøe Airlines Dash 8 and flew away to a remote airstrip, high in the still snow-covered mountains. We landed at Sogndal and then drove, far from the madding crowd, down the fir-clad

mountains, past the cascading waterfalls of melted snow to the tranquil road round the fjord named Sognefjorden. It snaked past the orchards of apples, the small but neat and fertile pastures, past the cinnamon- and saffron-coloured wooden houses with their neat lawns, ornate balconies and splendid, hanging baskets. High above us were the mountains, smoky blue and slate. Shafts of sunlight between the brooding clouds shot like lasers on to the silver water. We crossed Sognefjorden several times by ferry before we reached the Kviknes Hotel at Balestrand, a fine wooden edifice with balconies and towers, built on the water's edge at the head – or is it the foot? – of the fjord, where ferries ply between the brightly painted communities that dot the shores.

Spectacular waterfalls cascade from the mountains

Sognefjorden
Overworked? Stressed? Come
to Balestrand and get into
the Norwegian state of mind

Pilau Rice with Lamb or Goat

Despite the seemingly endless list of ingredients, this is a very simple dish to prepare. It is, after all, only an Indian-style paella. So, if you are making this dish for four or five friends it would be a good idea to invest in a paella dish (a shallow metal frying-pan 30-40cm/12-18 inches in diameter with small handles). Otherwise use a big wok or frying-pan with a lid – or a piece of foil.

Serves 6

100g (4oz) unsalted butter

$^1/_2$ teaspoon whole cloves

1 teaspoon green cardamom pods

$^1/_2$ teaspoon cumin seeds

2-3 bay leaves

1 onion, finely sliced

3-4 garlic cloves, finely chopped

1 tablespoon grated fresh root ginger

a couple of fresh chillies, deseeded and chopped

a couple of tablespoons of each of the following (mixed together) – ground
     nutmeg, ground cinnamon, ground cumin and ground coriander

a couple of tablespoons of vegetable oil

1kg (2lb 4oz) lean lamb or goat, trimmed and cubed

450g (1lb) basmati rice, rinsed and drained

1 teaspoon salt

150ml ($^1/_4$ pint) single cream

a big pinch of saffron strands, steeped in a little hot milk

50g (2oz) pine kernels, flaked almonds, cashew nuts or peanuts

50g (2oz) sultanas or raisins

50g (2oz) crystallized fruit (e.g. pineapple)

fresh coriander leaves

Begin by melting most of the butter in the pan and gently fry the cloves, cardamom pods, cumin seeds and bay leaves for 30 seconds or so, as this helps to release their flavours. Now add the onion, garlic, ginger and chillies, and stir-fry until they are soft – about 3-4 minutes.

Now add the mixture of ground spices. Mix well and fry gently for another minute. If the mixture has absorbed all the butter, add a couple of tablespoons of vegetable oil, so that you can fry the cubes of meat until they are browned in the spice and herb mixture. Take care not to burn any of the ingredients.

Next add the rice. Stir-fry it until it is well coated with all the ingredients. Season with salt, stir in the cream and saffron milk, and cover the whole lot with about 1.2 litres (2 pints), boiling water. Cover the pan with a lid or with foil, turn down the heat and simmer gently for about 15-20 minutes, or until the liquid has been absorbed, the rice is fluffy and the meat is cooked. If the rice isn't quite tender but the liquid has been absorbed add a little extra water and cook for a few minutes longer.

While the rice is cooking, melt the reserved butter in a frying-pan and add the pine kernels or nuts and sultanas or raisins, cooking them until they are slightly caramelized. Stir them into the main cooking pot along with the crystallized fruit. Sprinkle liberally with fresh coriander leaves.

Me and my new chums being filmed at Balestrand Goat Farm above Sognefjorden

PILAU RICE WITH LAMB OR GOAT KEBABS WITH SAFFRON YOGHURT

Make the pilau rice as in the previous dish, but without the lamb or goat, because you're going to serve the meat on kebabs instead, with a saffron-flavoured yoghurt.

Serves 6

For the kebabs
1 boned leg of lamb or goat
juice of 2 lemons
6 tablespoons olive oil
sprigs of fresh thyme or rosemary
salt and freshly ground black pepper

For the saffron yoghurt
a big pinch of saffron strands
2-3 tablespoons of milk
300ml (½ pint) thick whole-milk yoghurt

Remove the fat from the meat and cut it into 2.5cm (1 inch) cubes. Cut the meat into cubes of the same size. Thread the meat and the fat alternately on to skewers.

Mix the lemon juice and olive oil in a large, shallow container. Add the kebabs, rubbing the mixture all over them. Sprinkle with the sprigs of thyme or rosemary, and season with salt and pepper. Leave for a while (covered and chilled) until you are ready to cook them, and then barbecue or grill (or cook on a plancha) until tender and succulent – about 8-10 minutes or so.

Meanwhile, put the saffron into a little bowl or cup. Heat the milk until boiling, pour over the saffron and let it steep for at least 10 minutes. Strain into the yoghurt and mix well. Give each person a dollop of the pilau rice with the kebabs on top, pour over some saffron yoghurt and eat.

As night falls, the mountains grow black, and higher, and little ribbons of light from the villages flicker on, making a bracelet around the fjord as far as the eye can see. The view is breathtaking, the air is sweet and cool.

Of course, the next day, when we had to film, thick black clouds and swathes of mist had rolled over the distant mountains and suffocated the fjord. It was flat and grey and most distressing for the director, Mike, and the cameraman, Vlad the Impaler (whose real name, by the way, is Haakon, a Christian name favoured by the Norwegian royal family for ages). The whole crew hung around disconsolately waiting for the weather to break. It didn't – it rained instead. I planned to bake some cod in a rather elaborate way in a hitherto untried, wood-fired, mobile oven. I also planned to cook some Norwegian lobsters. Our attempts to get the wood oven up to frying speed were pathetic. One minute the dial was reading 'red – danger to machine', the next minute it had dropped back to 100°F. This cooker came highly recommended by my assistant Scott, who had assured me he had tested it thoroughly and it could smoke, roast, bake, grill, whatever 'with no trouble, guv!' After three hours of farting about, I was disinclined to concur. The trouble was, the baked cod dish was essential to the morning's cooking sketch and now I was on the back foot in front of the hotel chefs, the local press, curious guests, et al.

But help was at hand. Like the US cavalry arriving just in time in the good old westerns, a motorboat approached the hotel at high speed, its bow high out of the water. The skipper hit the harbour at twenty-five knots, slammed the motor astern and leapt ashore with a basket of the finest, fattest, all-singing, all-dancing, alive, alive-o langoustines – or as they say here, Norwegian lobsters – that you had ever seen in your life. We abandoned the amazing frying machine and quickly fired up my 50cm paella dish and through a flurry of olive oil, garlic, chillies and fresh tomato sauce, I created a modest culinary masterpiece! For those of you interested, I put some olive

Glorious Balestrand langoustines

oil into my very large paella pan, got it very hot and threw in the still kicking langoustines. I then added a load of finely chopped onion and garlic and stirred it around. I threw in half a handful of chopped-up dried chillies (fresh would have been better, but . . .), turned the langoustines over a couple of times and then flamed them in a massive slug of aquavit. As that burnt away, I poured in a litre or so of fresh tomato sauce, bubbled it for two or three more minutes, seasoned it with salt and pepper and threw over a handful of coriander leaves. You get really messy eating them, you might even burn your fingers, but they are jolly good.

Oh what a life! One day I was idly spinning for salmon from the stern of a magnificent vintage motor launch, the sort with the centre cockpit that is favoured by royalty when they alight from their yachts to go ashore, and the next I was humming 'A life on the ocean wave and a home on the foaming sea' at the helm of *Statsraad Lemkuhl*, a 321-foot, three-masted, square-rigged sailing boat commissioned in 1914 by Kaiser Bill as a training ship for the German navy and now used for adventure holidays, the sort where you pay lots of money to sleep in a hammock and blister your hands heaving ruddy great sails up and down while being shouted at by the permanent crew. Along with a hundred or so other similarly magnificent vessels, we were headed for Stavanger in the Cutty Sark Tall Ships Race. The captain ordered a change of course, bells rang, commands were shouted and eighty hands aged between seventeen and eighty-seven, chanting

For the weary mariner, Stavanger old town provides a great run ashore

and grunting, heaved on the massive sheets. The new course set safely for the night, we repaired to the captain's state room for a waffle party, which, as it turned out, had very little to do with waffles. (By the way, I love waffles smothered in fruity jam and thick cream, and have just purchased a waffle maker. The batter is very easy to make and the best recipe I have was given to me by Britt, the captain's wife. For ten people, mix together 3 eggs with 100g sugar, add a tablespoonful of vanilla sugar, half a teaspoon of baking powder, 200g of melted butter, a litre of buttermilk and a litre of ordinary milk and then whisk in some ordinary flour until you have a thick batter.)

'It was a hell of white water, the waves with teeth like bananas' quoth the ancient mariner

... Day 47 and the men and women aboard the good ship *Statsraad Lemkuhl* are getting restless. Surely we must sight a pub, oops, sorry, land soon

The secret of a successful waffle party, according to the chief steward, is how you amuse yourself between waffles; his solution was simple and effective, and was as follows. Ingredients: one fine walnut-panelled stateroom, one fine polished mahogany table, seven chairs, seven people, seven glasses, an able seaman to cook and serve the waffles, four bottles of brandy, one bottle of whisky. Method: combine all of the above gently for several hours, and then ask someone to help you to bed.

Curiously the movement of the vessel and the splendid atmosphere of the stateroom were more intoxicating than the alcohol and I leapt happily out of my bunk at 5.30 the next morning to set about preparing a chicken, mutton and chick-pea soup for the captain's and crew's lunch. Soon we were making our final run into Stavanger and the crew were busy swabbing the decks and hoisting hundreds of flags. The good ship *Statsraad Lemkuhl* was being dressed for the real party. Stavanger was in fiesta and the sun shone brightly on the charming wooden buildings. Church bells pealed, flags fluttered and jazz bands played as the magnificent vessels eased their way to their berths. Thousands filled the cafés and the bars while thousands more thronged the wharfs, munching bags of fresh prawns and cherries while watching the big ships come in. We fought our way through the crowds and set up shop on the quay. Surrounded by several hundred happy, curious souls, I cooked a huge stew of lobsters and fish in a garlic mayonnaise. They cheered delightedly at my every mistake and laughed raucously at my corny jokes. My goodness, what a contrast between this summer festival day in Stavanger, with its restaurants and bars – oh, and by the way if you ever stay at the Raddison in Stavanger, ask for the Atlantic Suite; it's great and quite different from the Seaman's Mission in Røst – anyway, what a contrast to those woeful frozen days we had spent in the north of Norway in the winter on the first leg of our journey, eating reindeer and drinking alcohol-free beer.

Here's one of me preparing my flagship dish – Stavanger lobster stew

STAVANGER LOBSTER AND FISH STEW

This is a party dish for those with a bent towards extravagance. You can use the lobster or crayfish, as many as you can afford, and you can use such fish as whole bream, whole red mullet, red snapper, big fillets of monkfish, small whole haddock or cod, in fact, any mixture of fish that you like with the exception of oily fish like herring or mackerel. Also, quantities and volumes are what you make them depending on the number you are feeding. So here is a fairly loose version of what I cooked on the quayside at Stavanger.

Serves 8

2 or 3 live lobsters or 1kg (2¼lb) crayfish

8 whole fish – not too big, and not oily, so avoid herring or mackerel. Choose from bream, red mullet, red snapper, small haddock, hake, etc., cleaned, scaled and de-finned

Garlic mayonnaise

2 bulbs of garlic, the cloves separated and peeled

4 egg yolks, plus 1 whole egg

pinch of salt

shake of white pepper

240ml (8fl oz) olive oil

Fish stew

2 onions, chopped

2 leeks, chopped

3 celery sticks, chopped

3 carrots, chopped

4-5 cloves garlic, chopped

a few parsley sprigs

a few fennel or dill fronds

a dozen or so black peppercorns

a tablespoon of sea salt

about 150ml (¼ pint) decent olive oil

a bottle of dry white wine

olive oil for frying

8 thick slices of crusty bread

about 3 tablespoons harissa (Moroccan chilli paste), for spreading

2kg (4½lb) potatoes, peeled and quartered

300ml (½ pint) double cream

a few saffron strands

First make the mayonnaise. In a food processor or blender, whizz the garlic to a paste and add the egg yolks and whole egg. Season with salt and pepper and add a drop or two of olive oil. Whizz again and then turn the machine on to high and slowly pour in the olive oil until you have a thick, yellow garlic mayonnaise.

Next start off the stew by half-filling a very large but fairly shallow cooking pot with water. Bring to the boil and then throw in the vegetables, garlic, herbs, peppercorns and salt. Add the olive oil and wine, and simmer for a while – 20 minutes or so.

In the meantime, make some chilli croûtons. Heat a generous slosh of olive oil in a frying-pan and fry the bread slices until lightly browned. Drain them on kitchen paper, spread lightly with the harissa paste and keep in a warm place. Put the potatoes on to boil.

Now cook the seafood. Plunge the lobsters in the boiling stock, put the lid on and cook for about 5-6 minutes. Remove them, cut them in half, crack the claws and keep in a warm place. If using crayfish cook for 4 minutes. Next add the whole fish to the stock and poach until cooked – about another 6 minutes. Test with a fork to make sure that the flesh is opaque and flakes easily.

Arrange the fish and lobsters or crayfish on a huge serving platter and keep warm in a low oven. Strain about 900ml (1½ pints) of fish stock into a saucepan and whisk in the cream over a low heat. Add the saffron strands and carry on whisking while you add the mayonnaise, giving you a rich, yellow sauce with the consistency of custard. Pour this over the fish, potatoes and lobster or crayfish. Pop the harissa croûtons on top and enjoy.

SALMON A LA PLANCHA

This recipe for griddled fish with a fresh herb salsa is served with saffron rice with dried fruits and nuts and a side dish of potatoes in mayonnaise. You can use it for salmon fillets, as here, or any other fish, whole or filleted.

A plancha is a flat steel or iron sheet that is heated over a gas flame. It forms a griddle surface on which you can cook anything, from fish or meat (chops, bacon, steaks, etc.) to eggs and vegetables and toasted bread. It gives an even, strong heat and a very quick result. Several things can be cooked at the same time on a plancha. You can also use it to keep food warm.

Serves 4

225g (8oz) long grain rice
a good pinch of saffron strands
sea salt
4 salmon fillets (150-175g / 5-6oz each)
a little oil
50g (2oz) stoned prunes, chopped
50g (2oz) dried apricots, chopped
25-50g (1-2oz) pine kernels or flaked almonds

A salmon freshly landed from an icy Norwegian river has an unparalleled flavour

110

Potatoes in mayonnaise

700g (1 1/2 lb) new potatoes

5 tablespoons fresh mayonnaise

about 1 tablespoon of capers, rinsed and chopped

about 1 tablespoon of chopped dill cucumber

salt and black pepper

Herb salsa

a good bunch of chopped fresh parsley

a good bunch of chopped fresh mint

1 red onion, finely chopped

3 or 4 tomatoes, skinned, deseeded and finely chopped

a good slosh of decent olive oil

juice of a couple of limes or 1 lemon

salt and freshly ground black pepper

Set your potatoes on to boil. Next, put the rice on to cook, along with the saffron strands (which will give it flavour and colour) and a good pinch of salt.

Meanwhile, make the herb salsa by mixing all the salsa ingredients together. Cover and refrigerate.

Make the sauce for the potatoes by combining the mayonnaise with the capers and dill cucumber, so that it ends up a bit like tartare sauce. Season with salt and black pepper.

Heat up the plancha – or use a griddle if you have one. Otherwise use a heavy-based frying-pan. Brush the salmon fillets on both sides with olive oil, and sear them on both sides on the plancha or in the pan. Season with a sprinkling of sea salt.

While the salmon is cooking, chuck the fruits and nuts on to the plancha (or into the pan) for a few seconds to toast them; then scoop them out and mix them into the cooked, drained rice. Mix the mayonnaise with the drained warm potatoes. The fish should be cooked after about 6-8 minutes; test it with a fork to make sure – the flesh should be opaque.

Now comes the easy bit. Lift the fish fillets on to warm plates, spoon over the salsa, serve with the saffron rice and potatoes – and eat.

COUSCOUS WITH FISH AND COCONUT SAUCE

I cooked this dish before a crowd of around 300 Saturday shoppers in Oslo, who questioned me at length about food and cooking and, of course, there was one who commented that this was not a Norwegian dish. I explained that the point of this exercise was not to teach them how to cook their own dishes, which they know perfectly well, but to do something a bit different and that this particular dish had its roots in Thailand, for the fish part, and Morocco for the couscous part. Anyway, it made a nice change from boiled cod!

Serves 4

1 fillet of mackerel or red mullet (or any firm
  fish you fancy) per person

juice of 2 lemons

3 tablespoons vegetable oil

1 onion, finely chopped

a couple of cloves of garlic, chopped

2 red or green chillies, deseeded and finely
  chopped

2 tablespoons Thai red or green curry paste

300ml (½ pint) coconut milk (buy this dried
  and reconstitute it, or buy it in a can)

a couple of lime leaves

a dash or two of Asian fish sauce (looks like
  soy sauce)

a wineglass of tamarind extract (buy some
  tamarind – from an Asian food supplier –
  soak it in hot water for a while and
  then squeeze the flesh to give you a liquid
  that looks like strong tea)

salt and freshly ground black pepper

a handful of chopped fresh coriander or basil,
  for garnish

For the couscous

50-75g (2-3oz) couscous (quick-cook) per person

a little oil

2 red peppers, deseeded and cut into chunks

50g (2oz) sultanas

50g (2oz) raisins or currants

50g (2oz) flaked almonds

a knob of butter

salt and freshly ground black pepper

Put the fish fillets into a shallow dish, squeeze over the lemon juice and leave to marinate for about 20 minutes or so.

Heat the oil in a sauté pan, frying-pan or wok, cook the onion, garlic and chillies for a couple of minutes and then stir in the curry paste. Mix well and cook gently for 2 minutes, then add the coconut milk, lime leaves, fish sauce, tamarind extract and finally, the fish fillets. Season with salt and pepper and cook gently until the sauce is creamy and the fish is cooked – about 10 minutes. If you prefer, you can grill the fish fillets, skin side up, for approximately 8 minutes, until the skin is nice and crispy brown.

While the fish is cooking, prepare the quick-cook couscous by pouring boiling water over it (check the pack instructions), stir with a fork and leave for a couple of minutes to swell up. Heat a little oil in another frying-pan, add the peppers and sear them for a few moments. Then chuck in the fruits and nuts, cooking them until they start to turn golden. Add the knob of butter to the couscous, stir it through to separate the grains, season it and mix in the toasted nuts, fruits and peppers.

To serve, place 3 spoonfuls of coconut sauce on to each plate, top with couscous and a fish fillet. Garnish, if you like, with coriander or basil and perhaps drizzle with some leftover sauce.

COUSCOUS WITH SHELLFISH

Prepare the coconut sauce as above, but instead of using fillets of fish, use scrubbed fresh mussels. You'll need a couple of pints of them at least. Chuck out any damaged ones, or ones that don't shut when tapped. Cook them in the sauce for about 2-3 minutes, this time throwing out any that don't open.

In the meantime, sear some fresh scallops on a lightly oiled plancha or griddle, or in a frying-pan or wok, for just a few moments. Season them with sea salt and then add them to the couscous. Ladle on to plates and spoon the mussels in coconut sauce on top.

POACHED HERRING FILLETS WITH DILL AND PARSLEY SAUCE

Serves 4

2 large carrots, diced

2 bunches of spring onions, trimmed and chopped

8 small fresh herring fillets

juice of 1 lemon

3 or 4 black peppercorns

salt

1 bay leaf

150ml (¼ pint) double cream

a good knob of butter

3 tablespoons chopped fresh parsley

3 tablespoons chopped fresh dill

Put the carrots and spring onions into a deep-sided frying-pan or large saucepan. Season the fish fillets, roll them up and position them on top of the vegetables. Add the lemon juice and enough water to just cover the fish. Add the peppercorns, a little salt and the bay leaf. Bring to simmering point and cook gently for 5 minutes. Lift the fish and vegetables on to a warmed serving platter and keep warm.

Bubble up the cooking liquid and boil it vigorously to reduce it down to about one-third of the original amount. Lower the heat and whisk in the cream. Now add the knob of butter and whisk again until slightly thickened. Strain through a fine sieve into another saucepan, add the parsley and dill and reheat gently. Check the seasoning, and pour over the fish and vegetables. Serve with plenty of buttery new potatoes.

NORWEGIAN POTATO WAFFLE WITH CAVIARS AND SOURED CREAM

Everywhere in Scandinavia there are waffles. Sweet ones served with jam and cream, or savoury ones, so I bought a waffle machine and let rip.

Serves 6 or so

Potato waffle
250g (9oz) self-raising flour
2 small eggs
120ml (4fl oz) single cream
300ml (½ pint) milk
100g (4oz) butter, melted and cooled
150g (6oz) potato, grated
salt and white pepper
vegetable oil for cooking

To serve
selection of salad leaves, lightly tossed in olive oil and lemon juice
100g (4oz) salmon caviar
100g (4oz) red lumpfish roe
100g (4oz) black lumpfish roe
100g (4oz) capelin roe
300ml (½ pint) thick soured cream
1 red onion, finely sliced
4 seagull's eggs (or plover's or quail's eggs) hard-boiled and halved

First prepare the waffle mixture: sift the flour into a large bowl, make a well in the middle and crack the eggs into it. Add the cream, milk and melted butter, and whisk together until you have a smooth batter. Beat in the potato and season well with salt and pepper. The batter should have the consistency of double cream. Cover and chill for 2 hours before using.

To make the waffles use a waffle iron, or cook them in some vegetable oil in a small, heavy-based frying-pan on both sides until golden brown. Put each waffle on the centre of a plate. Pile some lettuce leaves on to the middle of each waffle and put spoonfuls of the different caviars around the edge. Top with soured cream and red onion, and serve, garnished with the hard-boiled eggs.

Lamb and Chick-pea Soup

This dish is not native to Scandinavia but is from North Africa. My reason for preparing it in this way was purely practical. I had to cook a substantial, tasty, one-pot dish on the rolling deck of a 320-foot-long, four-masted schooner for around twenty people who had just come off an arduous watch, raising and trimming sails and frigging in the rigging.

Serves 4 or more

2 tablespoons olive oil
500g (1lb 2oz) fatty shoulder of lamb, diced
1 large onion, finely chopped
2-3 garlic cloves, crushed
a great big pinch of saffron strands
1 teaspoon ground ginger
loads of chopped fresh coriander
350g (12oz) carrots, cut into thick matchsticks
350g (12oz) courgettes, cut into thicker matchsticks
1 heaped tablespoon tomato purée
1 x 430g (15oz) can of chick-peas, rinsed and drained
salt and freshly ground black pepper

In a great big cooking pot, heat the oil and add the meat, a handful at a time, to sear and brown it. Add the onion and garlic and cook, stirring, for a minute or two. Stir in the saffron and ginger, along with a handful of the coriander. Pour in about 900ml (1½ pints) water, bring up to the boil and then reduce the heat; cover and simmer for about 50 minutes, or until the lamb is tender.

When the lamb is cooked, add the carrots and courgettes to the pan with the tomato purée. (You might need to add some extra water or meat stock.) Cook for a further 5-10 minutes. Meanwhile, purée the chick-peas in a blender or food processor. Tip them into the soup, stir and heat; then check the seasoning, adding salt and black pepper to taste. Serve with lots of coriander chucked on top.

BARBECUED OR DEEP-FRIED CHICKEN WITH LEMON SAUCE

This dish was inspired by the gift of a crate of lemon-flavoured vodka from a very generous Swedish wine merchant.

VERSION 1 – BARBECUED

1 poussin (very small chicken) per person

lemon juice

crushed garlic

fresh thyme

olive oil

salt and freshly ground black pepper

Lemon sauce

6 tablespoons or so of vodka – lemon-flavoured
   if possible

juice of 2 lemons

3-4 tablespoons clear honey

3-4 tablespoons of olive oil

a shake of salt

zest of 1 lemon

a few long strips of lemon zest, to garnish

Using a very sharp cook's knife, cut the poussins through the breast bone, as if you were cutting them in half, but don't cut right through – just splay them open, as if you were butterflying them. (When you start to do it, it will become clear.)

Rub the birds with lemon juice, crushed garlic, thyme and olive oil, and season them well with salt and pepper. Leave them in a cool place for an hour or so to absorb the flavours.

In the meantime, prepare a crunchy fresh salad with some mixed salad leaves, etc., and make a dressing to go with it. Then make the lemon sauce, whisking all the ingredients together – adding vodka and lemon juice to suit your taste – until it is fairly thick, but smooth.

Put some rice on to cook – either by boiling it in plenty of lightly salted water until tender, or by using a small electric rice cooker (which is well worth buying because the rice stays hot and perfect for up to 3-4 hours).

Cook the poussins either on the barbecue or under the grill – or, if you should be so fortunate to have one, on a plancha (a flat steel or iron cooking plate). It wants to be slightly burnt and crunchy on the outside and tender and succulent on the inside. Just before the end of the cooking time, garnish the poussins with the lemon zest strips so that they colour and release their flavour. Serve with the salad and rice, and a spoonful or so of the lemon sauce, which can be served either cold or warm.

VERSION 2 – DEEP-FRIED

1 skinless, boneless chicken breast per person
plain flour
salt and freshly ground black pepper
vegetable oil, for deep-frying
lemon sauce (see page 120)

Japanese tempura batter
100g (4oz) plain flour
½ teaspoon salt
2 teaspoons molasses sugar
1 teaspoon baking powder
3 tablespoons sesame oil
rice or cider vinegar

If the chicken breasts are quite large, slice them in two. Sprinkle the flour on to a plate, season it with salt and pepper, and lightly coat the chicken with it.

Make the Japanese tempura batter by whisking together the flour, salt, sugar, baking powder and sesame oil with 200ml (⅓ pint) of warm water and a shake of rice or cider vinegar. Chill in the refrigerator for 10-15 minutes.

Heat the vegetable oil. Dip the floured chicken into the batter, shaking off the excess, and deep-fry until crisp. Drain on sheets of kitchen paper to absorb the oil and neatly carve the fillets into bite-sized pieces.

Serve with rice and salad, as before, but this time make sure the lemon sauce is warm before you drizzle it over the chicken.

Food education for children is very important

FILLETS OF FISH A LA PLANCHA WITH ANCHOVY AÏOLI

Serves 4

4 firm white fish fillets (cod, halibut, haddock, etc.) trimmed into pieces measuring roughly 7.5cm (3 inches) square

plenty of olive oil

salt and freshly ground black pepper

lemon juice

4 thick slices of tomato bread (from the local deli or the bakery section in your supermarket)

Anchovy aïoli

50g (2oz) can anchovy fillets in olive oil

2 garlic cloves, crushed

3 free-range eggs

300ml (½ pint) olive oil

salt and freshly ground black pepper

For the tomato accompaniment

2 tomatoes, halved and deseeded

4 garlic cloves, crushed

lots of chopped fresh parsley

2 tablespoons olive oil

crunchy salad leaves, to serve

First of all, make the anchovy aïoli. Purée the anchovy fillets in a blender or food processor with the garlic, and then add the eggs, one at a time. Whizz for a few seconds, and then slowly drizzle in the olive oil while the motor is running to make a smooth mayonnaise, which only takes a few seconds. Season.

Next, fill the halved tomatoes. Mix together the garlic and chopped parsley with a little olive oil, and use this mixture to fill the tomatoes. Now heat a plancha (a flat steel or iron cooking plate) or use a heavy-based frying-pan, adding a little oil. Brush the fish squares with olive oil and sear them on both sides. Cook for about 5 minutes, seasoning them with a shake of salt, some black pepper and a squeeze of lemon juice.

While they are cooking, sprinkle the tomato bread on both sides with olive oil. Lift the fish squares out; sear the tomato bread pieces. Lightly fry the stuffed tomatoes, being careful not to let the filling fall out as you pick them up.

Put the slices of seared tomato bread on to four warmed plates. Top with the squares of fish, spoon on plenty of aïoli, pop a tomato half on each plate and serve with salad leaves.

BRAISED HAM WITH ROOT VEGETABLES AND PEA-GREEN SAUCE

Serves 4-6

1kg (2¼lb) gammon

600ml (1 pint) dry cider

a bouquet garni (parsley, thyme, bay leaf and peppercorns,
    tied up in a muslin bag)

175g (6oz) fresh or frozen petit pois

75ml (3fl oz) double cream

salt and freshly ground black pepper

450g (1lb) potatoes, scrubbed and diced

450g (1lb) carrots, scrubbed and diced

450g (1lb) turnips, scrubbed and diced

2 onions, peeled and cut into chunks

50g (2oz) butter

Put the gammon into a saucepan or flameproof casserole dish just big enough to contain it comfortably, and pour in the cider. Top up with enough cold water to cover, add the bouquet garni and bring to simmering point. Reduce the heat, pop the lid on and simmer gently for 1½ hours (30 minutes per 450g/1lb, plus 30 minutes). Lift the ham from the cooking pot, cover with foil and allow to rest.

Bubble up the ham stock and simmer without a lid until it has reduced down to about 150ml (¼ pint). Discard the bouquet garni.

Put the ham stock, peas and cream into a liquidizer or food processor and blend until smooth. Pour into a heatproof bowl and place over a saucepan of simmering water to keep warm. Stir often and season with salt and pepper.

Heat the butter in a frying-pan and tip in the diced vegetables, cooking them until they are nicely browned and crisp on the outside. Slice the ham thinly, and serve with the sautéed vegetables and pea-green sauce.

FRUIT-ALCOHOL-MARINATED SALMON WITH APPLE AND CHIVES

I am not a great fan of gravadlax but, undeniably, raw or marinated salmon is a quintessentially Scandinavian dish. So, here's another one.

Serves 4

1 piece of very fresh salmon, weighing around 350g (12oz)

1 wineglass of crème de cassis (about 120ml / 4fl oz)

a good dash of fruit-flavoured aquavit or vodka (with blackcurrant, blackberry or elderberry)

1 teaspoon of fine sea salt

a couple of grinds of coarse black pepper per portion

Apple salad

4 crisp eating apples

juice of ½ lemon

1 tablespoon chopped fresh chives

150ml (¼ pint) soured cream or crème fraîche

Get yourself a really sharp knife and cut the salmon into fine slices, about 6mm (¼ inch) thick. Mix together the marinade ingredients – the crème de cassis and aquavit or vodka, seasoning with a little sea salt and pepper. Pour over the salmon and leave at room temperature for about an hour, turning the salmon over from time to time.

Just before you want to eat, peel and core the apples, and then cut them into matchstick pieces, sprinkling them with lemon juice to stop them from going brown. Mix with the chives and soured cream or crème fraîche, and season.

Lift out the salmon, shaking off the excess liquid. Season with coarsely ground black pepper and a little sea salt and put a dollop of the apple mixture on top.

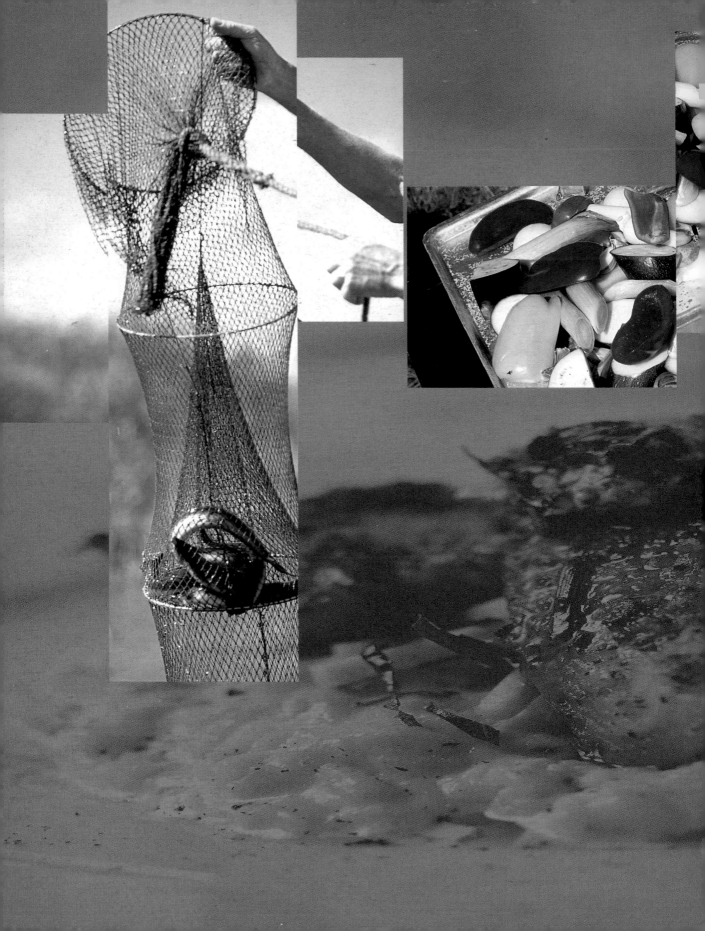

denmark

If the Scandinavian winters are horrendous, the summers are glorious, so on a fine summer's day, Mrs F and I, by now totally bored and frustrated with boats and planes and trains, commandeered the crew's Saab convertible to go to our next location, Mors in Denmark, a delightful journey, since Denmark was in mid-harvest: fat fields of swaying corn dotted with pretty, courtyarded farmhouses nestling beneath the slowly spinning blades of wind-driven electric generators. The Danish countryside is spectacularly flat, the highest landmark hereabouts, 150 metres, is called Sky Mountain. We broke our journey there for a picnic of freshly baked bread (universally good in Scandinavia), cold roast pork with plenty of fat and crisp crackling, pickled beetroot, dills and pickled cucumbers washed down with a couple of iced Pils that a man in a van thrust at me while we were stopped at traffic lights at seven o'clock that morning – a bizarre but typical reaction from the Scandinavian fans of my modest little programmes.

Left: The eel lake on Mors

Right: Practical, ecologically sound, but very sinister

131

Mors is an island in the north of Denmark where, on a farm museum called Skarregård, I spent an idyllic morning trapping eels in a reed-fringed lake with a local fisherman called Anton. Since neither of us could speak the other's language we communicated with a few shots of cherry brandy, which was a welcome pick-me-up after a harrowing ride, driving an antique, wooden-wheeled farm cart pulled by two mischievous Arctic ponies. At first the owner of these thoroughbreds had been reluctant to let me take the reins myself, but after a couple of trial runs, he was so impressed with my driving ability that he milked the mare, who had recently foaled, and proudly presented me with a tin mug, full to the brim with tepid horse milk, which I had no choice but to drink. I barely managed to avoid throwing up as I clambered on to the punt to

paddle out to the eel traps. I am not a great one for sticky drinks at nine in the morning so my cherry brandy was most welcome.

Anton and I chatted incoherently with each other, with smiles and nods as the only possible replies to what the other had said, and, after a couple of tranquil hours, we returned to the farm, where in front of astonished farm workers and about fifty members of the Danish press and media, I cooked the eels in red wine with bacon and onions, a sort of Eel au Vin. Eels, by the way (if they haven't been trapped by me) travel at night overland to the nearest river and then, by God knows what means of navigation, they set out for the Sargasso Sea where they lay their eggs 300-400 metres down in the ocean. The young then make their way back to the ponds and rivers; many will be netted as elvers and exported to the south of France and Spain, where they are considered a great delicacy, fried in olive oil with chillies and garlic.

Left: 'Surrey With A Fringe On Top'

Right: Eel fishing with Anton

EELS STEWED IN RED WINE

This is the kind of dish in which Curnonsky and Escoffier revelled and their wealthy customers devoured with pleasure.

Serves 4

700g (1½lb) freshwater eels, skinned and cut into 5cm (2 inch) lengths
    (preferably by your fishmonger)
50g (2oz) plain flour
salt and freshly ground black pepper
50g (2oz) butter, plus a bit more
100g (4oz) smoked streaky bacon, cut into 1cm (½ inch) pieces
16 small shallots or baby onions, peeled
16 button mushrooms
90ml (3fl oz) aquavit or cognac
1 bottle of red wine
1 tablespoon tomato purée
about a tablespoon of fresh thyme leaves or chopped parsley
2 bay leaves

Dredge the pieces of eel with the flour and season them with some salt and pepper. Melt the butter in a sauté pan – or use a wok. Fry the bits of bacon along with the shallots or onions until they start to turn golden brown. Turn the heat down really low and cook them for another 5 minutes or so.

Add another knob of butter to the pan and chuck in the eels and mushrooms, frying them until lightly coloured; then add the aquavit or cognac. Set a match to the mixture to flambé the alcohol, let the flames die away, pour in the bottle of red wine and stir in the tomato purée. Add the fresh thyme or parsley and bay leaves.

Simmer for about 45 minutes, without a lid, so that the liquid reduces down. Fish out the bay leaves, check the seasoning and serve with vegetables and potatoes.

Copenhagen:

Wonderful, Wonderful

Moving swiftly on, we headed for Copenhagen.

Wonderful, wonderful Copenhagen,

Friendly old girl of a town.

'Neath her tavern light

On this merry night

Let us clink and drink one down.

And this is the place to clink and drink several down, Copenhagen harbour.

WARM SMOKED EEL SALAD WITH CHILLED PARSLEY SAUCE AND SCRAMBLED EGGS

Eels and the Scandinavians go together like a horse and carriage. Smoked eel is widely available and delicious. However, I got the impression that I had put my foot in it when I innocently mentioned to one patriot that most of the breeding stock of their beloved eels came from Gloucestershire and Somerset!

Serves 4

1 bulb of celeriac, peeled and cut into
    matchstick pieces
a good handful of fresh mixed herbs (chives,
    parsley, dill, chervil, etc.), chopped
juice of $1/2$ lemon
4-5 tablespoons olive oil
salt and freshly ground black pepper
75g (3oz) butter
8 fillets of smoked eel
300ml ($1/2$ pint) best-quality lager (or as much
    as you fancy!)
4 eggs, beaten
a dash of milk

Combine the ingredients for the salad – in other words, the celeriac and the chopped mixed herbs. Add a good squeeze of lemon juice and drizzle over the olive oil. Season with salt and pepper, then cover and chill.

Next make the parsley sauce. Put the ingredients into a blender or food processor, whizz together for a few seconds, tip out into a jug, season and refrigerate.

Melt most of the butter in a frying-pan and put the rest into a non-stick saucepan. Bubble up the butter in the frying-pan, add the eel fillets and brown them on both sides. Add a good dash of lager and bubble for a couple of minutes or so. Quickly beat the eggs with the milk and scramble them in the other pan, but don't overcook them.

Serve the eel with the scrambled eggs, celeriac salad and chilled parsley sauce.

Arvid Muller, who wrote the song, must have been thinking of the pretty girls who pack the harbour bars. Blonde, tall, slim and friendly – I know this as some of my film crew told me at breakfast. This is a very lively place; the streets are packed from early morning till early the next morning, as I found out to my cost.

North Sea oil has been an economic boon to the country, giving Denmark one of the highest standards of living in the world. No wonder they are out all night celebrating.

A short bike ride from the harbour (where, by the way, bicycles are free to visitors in the way that supermarket trolleys are in supermarkets) is Christiania Freetown, where a different economic boom is taking place, the selling of hashish. This is where a couple of thousand bandana-wearing free spirits of all nationalities trade and smoke cannabis in a former military base with the blessing of the Danish government. It is Woodstock II, a manic Magic Roundabout where Zebedee still lives and Crosby, Stills and Nash blast from huge speakers. In this purple haze, faithfully following in the footsteps of the tambourine man, people crowded round my little set and pressed small packages of cannabis resin into my hand, pelted me with spliffs and adorned me with T-shirts that read 'Cannabis Can Save the World'. One of the elders explained that pedlars or users of hard drugs who attempt to ply their evil trade here are stripped, beaten up and thrown out. A man in a trenchcoat wanted eleven dollar bills for a box of magic mushrooms. I only had ten. Others gave me tickets for a star gig, a band called the Garlic Girls, who turned out to be a bunch of antipodean cross-dressers, but were highly entertaining nevertheless. People moved slowly between the hash and jewellery stalls, the air was heavy with dope and life was in slo-mo; the sun was seriously hot and

Left: The quays are where it's at in summer

Right: Christiania Freetown. For some, it is the pot (ha-ha) of gold at the end of the rainbow

the camera had broken and I sat on the tailgate of our truck chopping chives and sipping wine to the beat of bongo drums and sometimes posed for a photograph with people saying, 'Hey man, what are you doing here?' and I was thinking, 'Ain't it clear I can't stay in here?' and the afternoon ground on. 'Tell the world please, we don't mean no harm and, besides, we pay taxes now and are Copenhagen's second biggest tourist attraction next to the Tivoli Gardens, and pot doesn't do you any harm and I've been here for fifteen years, man, ain't it clear that we like it here and no businessmen drink our wine and no ploughmen dig our earth. If anybody is wondering it's too bad because they know nothing about how much any of this is worth.'

As I cooked they were swaying, they clapped, they cheered, they ate the food, they took me into their homes with polished floors and hi-fis, they made me tea and fed me cake and said 'Hey man, thanks for coming here.' I wondered whether Dougal, Dillon and Florence were still having honey for tea as I boarded my taxi and fled for the Michael Jackson concert with the very special tickets given to me last night by his chauffeur.

Poached Halibut with Steamed Vegetables and Green Pea Sauce

It was truly in the corner of a foreign field that I prepared this delightful summer meal in front of a pot-induced, bemused audience in Copenhagen's Christiania Freetown. Rudyard Kipling's immortal words, 'If you can keep your head when all about you are losing theirs' spurred me on to cook on the raised wooden sidewalk that will be for ever England.

Serves 4

4 x 175g (6oz) pieces of halibut fillet, skinned

about 600ml (1 pint) fish stock, for poaching

about 2 teaspoons of freshly grated raw horseradish (if you can get it)

some fresh spinach leaves, deep-fried until crispy, to garnish (optional)

For the vegetables

2 large carrots, cut into 7.5cm (3 inch) batons

4 celery sticks, cut likewise

1 bulb of fennel, ditto

100g (4oz) fine green beans

100g (4oz) mangetout

2 bunches spring onions, trimmed and sliced into long strips

100g (4oz) asparagus spears

lots of long fresh mint sprigs, for tying (or use chives)

For the green pea sauce

175g (6oz) frozen petits pois, defrosted

25g (1oz) butter

2 tablespoons double cream

1 tablespoon chopped fresh mint

salt and freshly ground black pepper

First prepare your vegetables. You are going to tie them into neat little bundles, so group together some little piles of carrot, celery and fennel, and some piles of green beans, mangetout, spring onions and asparagus. Use the mint sprigs to wrap around the bundles and tie them securely. (Chives should do the trick too.) Put the vegetables into a steamer and steam for 10 minutes until cooked, yet crunchy.

Meanwhile, put the petits pois into a saucepan and heat with the butter. Purée them in a blender or food processor and return to the saucepan. Heat gently.

Next, put the fish fillets into a large frying-pan and add the fish stock and horseradish. Heat and simmer for about 5 minutes, until the fish is cooked –

the flesh will flake easily when tested with a fork. Remove the fish and keep it in a warm place.

Now quickly finish off the pea sauce. Add a spoonful or so of the fish cooking liquor to the puréed peas, along with the cream and chopped mint. Heat gently, stirring until you have a smooth, creamy sauce. Season to taste.

Spoon some of the pea sauce on to warm serving plates, place the halibut on top and sprinkle with grated horseradish. Surround with bundles of steamed vegetables and garnish with the spinach leaves, if using.

Above and centre:
Only the best will do for this
delicious cherry liqueur

Above right:
Mr Heering's family crest

Just outside Copenhagen there is a large and beautiful cherry orchard, where, some years ago, a certain Mr Heering perfected the art of making a splendid cherry-flavoured alcohol, known the world over as Cherry Heering. Beneath the blood-red-laden boughs in this orchard of joy, still reeling and free-wheeling from my afternoon in Christiania Freetown's Woodstock Café, I prepared smoked loin of pork with a cherry sauce for the timid and shy white-coated cherry pickers before moving on to Kronborg Castle, at Hälsingør.

SMOKED LOIN OF PORK IN BLACK-CHERRY SAUCE

Lightly smoked loin of pork is a Danish delicacy. Look out for it at your local specialist shops or supermarkets, or use pork fillet – or even wild boar – instead.

Serves 4

50g (2oz) butter

about 12-16 thin slices of smoked pork loin (weighing about
    375-450g/12-16oz)

2 shallots, finely chopped

a couple of tablespoons of Cherry Heering liqueur,
    cherry brandy or brandy

200ml (⅓ pint) red-wine sauce, with a veal or chicken base
    (or use half red wine and half stock)

100g (4oz) fresh black cherries, pitted

a few leaves of fresh thyme

zest of 1 lemon, finely shredded

salt and freshly ground black pepper

Why do the French sneer at the English for eating apple sauce with roast pork? Everyone knows pork and fruit are symbiotic, and these succulent cherries are no exception

Heat the butter in a frying-pan and add the slices of pork loin. Sauté them lightly for about a minute on each side and then add the chopped shallots. Pour in the alcohol, flame it with a match, and let it die down. Remove the meat, and keep it in a warm place.

Add the red-wine sauce to the pan and stir everything together; then add the cherries. Heat for a few moments, and add the thyme leaves and lemon zest. Check the seasoning and pour over the meat.

Hamlet or Ham Omelette?
That is the question,
because this blasted wood
burning stove defeated me

Shall we dance?
The majestic interior of
Kronborg Castle

Kronborg Castle is located at the narrow sound separating Denmark from Sweden. This fortified Renaissance castle is four hundred years old and, except for playing bit parts in occasional wars against Sweden, its main purpose was to control the pirates and smugglers plying their nefarious trade through the narrow inlet. Large parts of Shakespeare's *Hamlet* were set in the castle. In the play, as of course you know, the young prince of Denmark is commanded by the ghost of his father to avenge his death, and it all ends dramatically with the death of the main protagonists.

Beside the castle walls, I prepared typical Danish roast pork and partridge for Rosencrantz and Guildenstern (who else), but, needless to say, like Hamlet, they failed to turn up, so I served the food to the crew and read Hans Christian Andersen's 'The Princess and the Pea', a tale more accessible and digestible than Shakespeare's drama; as Hamlet said, 'A man may fish with the worm that hath eat of a king, and eat of the fish that hath fed of that worm.'

The rooftops of Copenhagen

Above: The spire
of Vor Frelsers church

Right: The Changing
of the Guard

sweden

There are some ninety thousand lakes in Sweden, most of them full of superb freshwater fish – pike, perch, zander and bream. The waters are so clear that the Swedes are proud to tell you that you can fish for salmon in the centre of Stockholm. Many of the lakes are linked by rivers or canals and a perfect way to see the countryside is by boat.

So, on a hot summer's day, I boarded the *Juno*, a 120-year-old former postal and cargo ferry, now a lovingly restored luxury passenger boat plying the Göta Canal, and sailed through the Swedish lakes, days, canals and nights for Stockholm, 'The Venice of the North'. We chugged gracefully along the reed-fringed canals with the quaint, neatly painted lock-keeper's cottages, in and out of the myriad of little islands, lazing on the aft deck, aperitif in hand, trying to gather the strength for the next excellent meal. The highlight of the trip for me happened to be the simple but delicious Swedish Summer Soup created by the ship's chef, Emanuel Augustin (see recipe on page 186).

Left: Freshwater fishing is a very important industry

Right: Swedish rivers are a paradise on earth for anglers

Before I joined the *Juno*, I spent an idyllic couple of days fishing for pike, bream and zander at Skarblacka. The Swedes, sensibly, appreciate the very delicate flavours of freshwater fish unlike, say, in the UK where it is probably only salmon and trout that are appreciated. So, I had huge fun

Above: Typical Swedish

lakeside summer house

Left: The good ship *Juno*

in the Göta Canal

cooking freshwater bream Chinese-style, cooking perch in a tandoori marinade, making Thai fish soup and much more. The freedom of applying these exotic, but relatively simple, cooking techniques to such an easily accessible and wide variety of Swedish ingredients gave some great results.

The tranquillity of the river fishing was in stark contrast to a hot August night later in the week when, at a lake at Orkeljunga, we spent a mad, gleeful time with music, dancing and raucous singing. This is the only night in the year when the Swedes can indulge one of their great passions: catching, cooking and eating freshwater crayfish. We bobbed about in little boats with lamps hauling in these delicious crustacea. The traditional Swedish way is to boil them in a mixture of water, beer and aquavit, flavoured with dill and eaten cold, possibly with mayonnaise. But, the festivities on the lakeshore, with the accordions, drums, guitars, folk-songs, odes, funny hats, lanterns and costumes, fancy dress and all, reminded me of a night I spent on a bayou in Louisiana, so I cooked the crayfish Cajun-style, much to the amused delight of my hundred or so fellow revellers.

They partied on until dawn while we motored south in a splendid turbo-charged Saab convertible to an elegant country house hotel, Kronovoll, where, apart from running a fine kitchen, Anders Åkesson is Sweden's only sparkling winemaker. Swedish sparkling wine, I hear you cry. Surely, there's no such thing! But, my dear gastronauts, there is. With great vinous and entrepreneurial skill, Anders Åkesson imports the grapes from Italy and makes the wine on his estate. And damn fine stuff it is too.

During a lull in filming, I spent a couple of happy hours fishing on his lake. For all the world, I could have been in the Dordogne or in Tuscany. It then crossed my mind that an establishment such as this in either of those two places (or, indeed, in any other wine-producing region) would entertain the workers to a great feast after the winemaking had finished. A goose paddled by and inspired a Swedish version of a typical *vendange*; the Spanish *Cocida* or the Italian *Bollito*: a slow, simmering *mélange* of wonderful Swedish smoked sausages and bacon, ham, goose, chicken with dried white beans, carrots, artichoke hearts, leeks, onions and cabbage along with two or three cloves of garlic, a load of fresh parsley, a couple of sprigs of thyme and, of course, salt and pepper. This is not exactly a recipe for cooking at home, but if ever you do feel like taking a twenty litre or so pot and simmering all of these wonderful things for twenty or thirty friends then it's a great little recipe!

And so, on the good ship *Juno* we made our final approach to the spectacular harbour of Stockholm. The impressive tall ships, buzzing water ferries zapping to and fro, the myriad of floating restaurants, the quayside hustle and bustle and the fine architecture of its imposing buildings make this the most cosmopolitan of cities. And it was so hot!

Lunch that day in my Stockholm hotel, the very fine Diplomat, although one of the simplest dishes I have eaten anywhere, was unquestionably among the best I have ever tasted. It was a firm, milk-white fillet of fresh halibut, gently poached, smothered in melted butter and topped with grated horseradish. Accompanied by perfect mashed potato, pushed through a ricer to create little noodle-like shapes, this was an easy, fresh and delicious dish (see the recipe on page 176).

Stockholm, the 'Venice of the North'

A superb party dish ...

... but sadly these freshwater
crayfish are becoming
more and more scarce

FRESHWATER SWEDISH CRAYFISH BOILED LOUISIANA-STYLE

Serves 12

12 medium potatoes, scrubbed, but not peeled

12 small red onions, peeled

12 fresh corn on the cob, cut in half

6 oranges, halved

6 lemons, halved

6 heaped tablespoons Cajun seasoning (check the spices
    in your local supermarket)

4 bottles of strong lager

1 bottle of aquavit

salt and freshly ground black pepper

8-10 live crayfish per person (96-120 in total!)

100g (4oz) butter

Put all the vegetables, fruit and Cajun seasoning into a whacking great cauldron. Tip in the lager and aquavit, add enough water to cover the whole lot and season with about a tablespoon of salt.

Put the pot on to a fierce heat and bring to the boil, stirring occasionally to mix in the spice. Cook for about 20 minutes over a reduced heat until the potatoes are almost tender, chuck in the live crayfish and continue to cook until they are bright red in colour.

Fish out the cooked crayfish and pile them on to a huge serving platter. Remove all the vegetables and fruit, put them on another huge platter and smother in butter and plenty of freshly ground black pepper.

Below: The beautiful formal
gardens at Kronovoll Castle

Right: The harvest

Left: Me and Anders Åkesson

Above: A slow, simmering *mélange* of smoked sausages, bacon, ham, goose and vegetables

Below: A goostronomic get-together

Left: Kronovoll Castle in Southern Sweden is an elegant country-house hotel in a beautiful lakeside setting, and the proprietor, Anders Åkesson, makes excellent sparkling wine from grapes that he imports from Italy. He regularly has wine-tasting parties and gastronomic get-togethers

I was sipping a beer and nibbling prawns in a harbour-side café watching the water taxis jetting in and out between the regal tall ships, schooners and brigantines. The water festival was in full swing; the streets, the squares, the cafés, the jetties and the quays were crowded with exuberant merrymakers. In the soft warm night the air was filled with the music of thirty or forty concerts from Credence Clearwater Revival or, to be exact, John Fogerty and his band, to Vivaldi and old Dixieland jazz. A cavalcade of outrageously finned, chromium-plated pink and lime-green American classic cars cruised the streets, horns blaring, radios roaring, drivers and passengers waving and drinking, smiling, shouting in the joy of this summer Stockholm fiesta.

There was a Pinter play at the national theatre just down the street from my hotel and roller-bladers glided and swerved through the waiting theatre-goers. Trams and articulated buses ground by and the American cars came round again for the third time as Mrs F and I, spoilt for choice of restaurants, tossed a coin. The Japanese restaurant won and we ate sushi on the sidewalk on this hot August night, as crocodiles of tourists followed their placard-waving leaders through the ancient streets.

Right: Blondes on bicycles. Yippee!

Far right: 'A soldier's life is terrible hard,' said Alice

Stockholm ... On the waterfront

Above: Stockholm, Sunday.
A musical performance worthy
of Broadway

Above right: What's paella
got to do with it?

Left: '... Really hard,' said Alice

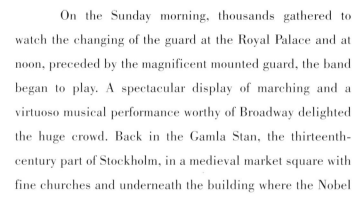

On the Sunday morning, thousands gathered to watch the changing of the guard at the Royal Palace and at noon, preceded by the magnificent mounted guard, the band began to play. A spectacular display of marching and a virtuoso musical performance worthy of Broadway delighted the huge crowd. Back in the Gamla Stan, the thirteenth-century part of Stockholm, in a medieval market square with fine churches and underneath the building where the Nobel committee presides, I cooked a Scandinavian paella and chicken with almonds and honey in front of a bemused crowd of multinational tourists. It is said that archaeological excavation has proved that ladies' high-heeled shoes were invented in Stockholm because, in the Middle Ages, garbage and refuse thrown into the square was so thick that high-heeled shoes were a necessity in order to avoid the unavoidable. My cooking sketch was finished, the dish had been devoured and my mind was drifting, absorbing the atmosphere of the square, when I heard a voice. 'Gee, these cardboard houses look just like the back lot of Twentieth Century Fox; was it the *Mary Poppins* set we saw, Wilma?'

Just when I was really enjoying myself, it was time to move on. Another day, another dinner, another airport.

CHICKEN WITH ALMONDS AND HONEY

A summer Sunday morning in Stockholm city. What dish could be more pleasant than chicken cooked with almonds and saffron in front of the headquarters of the Nobel Prize committee? Answers on a postcard.

Serves 4

4 tablespoons olive oil

1 large free-range chicken, jointed into small pieces

generous pinch of saffron strands

1 tablespoon grated fresh root ginger

salt and freshly ground black pepper

300ml (½ pint) chicken stock

75g (3oz) butter

3 large onions, sliced

1 teaspoon ground cinnamon

a generous dollop of honey

100g (4oz) blanched almonds

chopped fresh parsley or coriander, to garnish

Heat the olive oil in a large, deep-sided frying-pan or saucepan and fry the chicken pieces for about 10 minutes, until the outside is crispy and golden brown. Add the saffron and ginger, and some salt and pepper, and stir-fry for a couple of minutes. Pour in the stock, bring to the boil, cover and reduce the heat. Cook gently for about 30 minutes or so, checking occasionally to see that there is enough liquid and adding a bit more stock if it looks at all dry.

Meanwhile, melt most of the butter in a frying-pan and cook the onions until golden brown and caramelized – about 15 minutes. Stir in the cinnamon and honey, cook for a few moments and tip into the chicken pot; mix everything together and cook for a minute or two. Sauté the almonds in the remaining butter for a couple of minutes, seasoning them with a shake of salt.

Scatter the almonds over the chicken and garnish with the chopped herbs. Serve with iced lemon courgettes. (See page 189.)

Bikes, blades,

blondes, babes and

men in frocks

Gamla Stan (old town)
boasts some fine architecture
from across the centuries

FLOYD'S FRESHWATER FISH FIESTA

One of the highlights of my journey in Sweden was being presented with bulging nets of flapping freshwater fish on the river at Skarblacka. I had a riotous time cooking dishes from all over the world while gliding past the reeded banks in a flat-bottomed aluminium boat, laden to the gunnels with makeshift steamers, my plancha and a wok. Needless to say, seafish can happily replace any of the freshwater ones in the following five recipes. Each serves 4 generously.

ZANDER WITH PIQUANT SAUCE

1 thick fillet of pike or zander (weighing about 700g (1½lb)

3 tablespoons olive oil

3-4 teaspoons piri-piri seasoning or crushed dried chillies

Relish for the pike or zander

3 tablespoons olive oil

1 red pepper, deseeded and diced

1 small onion, finely chopped

1 tablespoon grated fresh ginger

1 garlic clove, crushed

3-4 hot red chillies, deseeded and finely chopped

1 small can chopped tomatoes

1 tablespoon dark muscovado sugar

a dash of red wine vinegar

salt and freshly ground black pepper

First make the relish. Heat the olive oil in a small saucepan and add all the relish ingredients. Bring up to the boil, reduce the heat and simmer for about 20 minutes or so, until reduced to an almost chutney-like consistency. Season with some salt and pepper, and then chill.

To cook the fish, brush with olive oil and sprinkle with the piri-piri seasoning or dried chillies. Grill until it is cooked, when the fish will be opaque and the flesh flakes easily – about 10 minutes. Serve sliced into four with the relish.

TANDOORI PERCH

2 plump fillets of perch
150ml (¼ pint) natural yoghurt
1 tablespoon tandoori powder
a couple of tablespoons cold water

Relish for the tandoori perch
½ small cucumber, finely chopped
2 tablespoons chopped fresh mint
150ml (¼ pint) natural yoghurt

Put the fish into a shallow dish. Mix together the yoghurt, tandoori powder and water. Pour over the fish, cover and leave to marinate for an hour or so. To make the relish, just mix together the relish ingredients and chill thoroughly.

Grill the fish for about 4-5 minutes on each side, making sure that it is cooked by testing it with a fork. (The fish should flake easily and the flesh should look opaque.) Slice each fillet in two and serve with the relish.

POACHED HALIBUT WITH HORSERADISH

This is one of the simplest dishes in the entire book and yet, for me, it is one of the most delicious.

1 thick piece of skinned and boned halibut per person

fish stock, for poaching (about 600ml/1 pint for four people)

melted butter (about 75g/3oz for four people)

enough creamed mashed potato for a decent portion for everyone

freshly grated horseradish – a teaspoon or so per person

a sprig of fresh dill per person

a wedge of lemon per person

salt and freshly ground black pepper

Put the halibut fillets into a suitable vessel with the fish stock and poach them gently for a few minutes – about 5 or 6 – until the flesh is opaque and the fish flakes easily when prodded with a fork.

Pour some melted butter on to warmed serving plates, and then, using a potato ricer (if you have one – it's a clever gadget that produces finely milled mashed potato), squeeze a portion of mashed potato on to each of the plates. Place a fish fillet on top of each serving, sprinkle with some finely grated horseradish (be generous) and finish off with a sprig of dill, a wedge of lemon and some salt and coarsely ground black pepper.

Cooking freshwater fish on the river at Skarblacka

STEAMED BREAM WITH BLACK BEAN SAUCE

1 plump bream, weighing about 700g (1½lb), cleaned and scaled

a dash of sesame oil

salt and freshly ground black pepper

1 carrot, cut into fine (julienne) strips

½ red pepper, deseeded and cut into fine strips

½ green pepper, deseeded and cut into fine strips

3-4 spring onions, trimmed and sliced into fine strips

5cm (2 inch) piece of fresh root ginger, peeled and
    sliced into thin strips

2 garlic cloves, thinly sliced

75g (3oz) Chinese black beans (see below)

1 red or green chilli, deseeded and cut into strips

oyster sauce, to taste

If you have a fish kettle you can use it for this recipe. If not, improvise by using a roasting pan with a trivet or a grill pan with a couple of sheets of foil.

Rinse the fish and rub sesame oil all over it. Season it with salt and pepper.

Next, pour some water – about 1.2-1.8 litres (2-3 pints) – into your fish kettle, roasting pan or grill pan. Put the trivet in place (in the fish kettle or roasting pan), and in the case of the grill pan, cover the grill rack with foil with a few holes poked in it. Now put the carrot, peppers, spring onions, ginger, garlic, black beans and chilli on the trivet.

Place the fish on top and cover with the lid – or another sheet of foil. Lift on to the hob and heat, probably using two rings of your cooker, until the water is steaming vigorously. Turn down the heat just a little and steam the fish briskly for about 15-20 minutes until it is cooked – the flesh should be opaque, and should flake easily when tested with a fork.

Carefully lift the fish and vegetables on to a warm serving platter. Save any juices that come out to use in a fish soup, stock or sauce. Serve the fish, topped with a few drops of oyster sauce – and there you have it!

NB. Chinese black beans are fermented black soya beans preserved in salt and ginger. You can buy them dried, which are best, from oriental food suppliers. Otherwise look out for canned ones – be sure to rinse and drain them first.

LEMON PEPPER PERCH

2 plump fillets of perch

3 tablespoons olive oil

juice of 1 lemon

2 tablespoons crushed white peppercorns

Relish for the lemon pepper perch

juice of 1 lemon

juice of 1 lime

200ml (1/3 pint) home-made (or good-quality) mayonnaise

segments of 1 lemon, 1 lime and 1 orange, with pith removed

First make the relish by whisking the lemon and lime juice into the mayonnaise; add the lemon, lime and orange segments. Stir well and then chill thoroughly.

Cook the fish under the grill, first brushing it with olive oil and then with lemon juice mixed with the crushed peppercorns. It will need about 4-5 minutes under a medium-hot grill, depending on its thickness. Check that it is done, as before. Slice each fillet in two and serve with the relish.

SWEDISH HASH

This popular and tasty dish is served all over the place; many a time, after long days of filming in Scandinavia, too tired to face another restaurant meal, we would have this in our room while we watched the telly or typed out the recipes for this book. It is a very versatile dish because it can be made happily either with fresh ingredients, e.g. very small cubes of fillet steak, raw potato and onion, or with cubes of left-over boiled potatoes and, say, left-over cold roast lamb. It also works well with bacon.

For each person

a good knob of butter, for frying
1 small onion, chopped
1 large potato, cut into tiny cubes
1 fillet steak, cut into cubes
a dash of Worcestershire sauce
salt and freshly ground black pepper
chopped fresh dill and parsley
1 free-range egg yolk

Melt the butter in a heavy frying-pan, add the onion and cook until nicely browned. Remove from the pan with a draining spoon, add a bit more butter to the pan and cook the potato until browned and tender. Lift the cubes from the pan too. Now add the steak and cook over a high heat for a few moments.

Whack the onion and potato back into the pan, mix everything together and add a dash of Worcestershire sauce (if you wish). Season with salt and pepper; then pile on to your plate and scatter the dill and parsley on top. Sit a raw egg yolk in its shell in the centre of the hash, ready to stir in just before eating. If you're not keen on the idea of a raw egg yolk, a freshly fried egg tastes just as good.

FLOYD'S HAMBURGER WITH SPICED ONION RELISH

You cannot travel the length and breadth of Scandinavia without encountering the ubiquitous meatball. These golf-ball-sized bullets of over-minced veal, pork or beef appear to be served with a variety of powdery, packet sauces. There is a white sauce, a red-coloured sauce and a brown-coloured sauce, and sometimes there is a reddish-brown-coloured sauce with lumps in it. Even the locals regard them as something of a joke, but at the same time they are very much part of the culinary culture. You cannot hide from the meatball! And, if a meatball doesn't get you then a chewy kind of meat patty will. And, if both of those culinary Exocets fail to find their way on to your plate, then a piece of meatloaf or a hamburger will. So, instead of attempting any of the above, I offer you my hamburger with spiced onions.

For each person

175-225g (6-8oz) prime minced sirloin steak

salt and freshly ground black pepper

melted butter

Spiced onion relish

2 tablespoons olive oil

a knob of butter

2 large onions

2 garlic cloves, finely chopped

2 tablespoons chopped fresh parsley

3 tablespoons chopped fresh coriander

a good pinch of ground cinnamon

1 teaspoon grated fresh root ginger

a good pinch of hot paprika

a few saffron strands

1 teaspoon cumin seeds

juice of 1 or 2 lemons

2-3 tablespoons honey

50-75g (2-3oz) raisins

salt and freshly ground black pepper

First make the relish. Heat the oil and butter together and then sauté the onions until they are golden. Add everything else to the pan, seasoning well with salt and black pepper. Cook over a low heat for about 6-8 minutes; cool and chill before serving.

To make the burgers, season the meat with salt and pepper. Shape into burgers and brush both sides with melted butter. Heat a heavy frying-pan without adding any oil. Slap the burgers into the pan and sear for about 1½ minutes on both sides. Put on to hot plates, season with a bit more salt and black pepper and pile a great dollop of spiced onions on top of each one. (No need for soggy buns, coleslaw, ketchup or mustard. And by the way, the spiced onions make a brilliant accompaniment to any grilled meat or fish.)

The ubiquitous meatball ...

found in the best hotels

EMANUEL AUGUSTIN'S SWEDISH SUMMER SOUP

Serves 4-6

1.2 litres (2 pints) milk

1 onion, studded with a couple of cloves

a sprig of fresh parsley

a couple of bay leaves

50g (2oz) butter

50g (2oz) plain flour

¼ cauliflower, broken into small florets

2 carrots, cut into thin slivers

1 large leek, shredded

100g (4oz) mangetout, sliced

1 bunch spring onions, trimmed and sliced

100g (4oz) dwarf green beans, sliced

1 tablespoon coriander seeds, crushed

2 teaspoons of fresh thyme leaves

1 tablespoon chopped fresh parsley

½ teaspoon cayenne pepper

150ml (¼ pint) double cream

salt and freshly ground black pepper

Put the milk into a large saucepan and add the onion, parsley and bay leaves. Bring it slowly to the boil – watch out that it doesn't boil over. Switch off the heat and allow the flavours to infuse for 15 minutes. Strain the mixture and discard the onion and herbs.

Melt the butter in another pan over a low heat. Stir in the flour and cook gently for a minute or two. Gradually add the flavoured milk, stirring to incorporate, and heat gently, stirring all the time to make a smooth, thin, creamy sauce. Next add all the vegetables and cook for about 5 minutes until they are *al dente*. Stir in the crushed coriander, thyme, parsley, cayenne and cream. Finally add the well-drained vegetables. Season with salt and pepper, make sure it's piping hot, and ladle into soup bowls.

RICE WITH RABBIT AND SHELLFISH

Serves 4-6

5-6 tablespoons of olive oil

1 rabbit, jointed into 8 pieces

1 large onion, coarsely chopped

1 red pepper, deseeded and cut into strips

4-5 garlic cloves, crushed in their skins

350g (12oz) Arborio (risotto) rice

salt and freshly ground black pepper

about 1.5 litres (2½ pints) chicken stock or water

a very generous pinch of saffron strands

18-20 live mussels, washed and scrubbed to remove beards (throw away any
    that remain open when tapped)

18-20 clams, well scrubbed (chuck out any that remain open)

a dozen large raw prawns or langoustines

100g (4oz) frozen peas

In a very large frying-pan or wok, heat the olive oil and fry the pieces of rabbit until crispy and golden brown. Add the onion, pepper and garlic, cook for a couple of minutes, stirring often, and then add the rice. Keep stirring for another 2 minutes or so until all the grains are coated in oil. Season with salt and pepper.

Pour in enough stock or water to just cover the ingredients. Add the saffron strands, pop on the lid or cover with foil and cook over a low heat for about 20 minutes, checking that the pan doesn't boil dry – add more stock or water if necessary.

Tip the mussels, clams and prawns or langoustines into the pan. Cover once more and cook for about 10 minutes, so that the steamy heat cooks the shellfish, causing the mussels and clams to open – discard any that don't. Leave on the heat for a couple of minutes until you have a crunchy, slightly golden crust on the bottom of the rice. Add the peas and cook for 2 minutes, just before serving.

ICED LEMON COURGETTES

Something different, I feel, for the ubiquitous courgette.

Serves 4

3 lemons

4-5 medium courgettes, sliced into batons about 2.5cm (1 inch) long

1 medium onion, very finely sliced

about 150ml (¼ pint) chicken stock

1 heaped tablespoon white sugar

1 tablespoon grated fresh root ginger

a dash of sesame, hazelnut or walnut oil

salt and freshly ground black pepper

chopped fresh parsley

Using a sharp serrated knife, remove all the peel and pith from the lemons. Cut them into segments, removing all the membrane (like grapefruit segments). Now put them into a saucepan with all the other ingredients, apart from the parsley, and bring up to simmering point. Cook gently for 15-20 minutes, stirring from time to time. Season to taste and chill before eating. Add some parsley just before serving.

greenland

The world's largest island looks like an awesome, abandoned and unworked quarry covered by almost two million square kilometres of ice, which is in places up to four kilometres thick. The perfect location for making a sci-fi Martian movie or for training astronauts to moon-walk. However, the coast, with its magnificent mountains, fjords, glaciers and icebergs, is breathtakingly beautiful and attracts thousands of hikers, botanists, fishermen, naturalists, geologists, mountaineers, adventurers and the plain crazy, not to mention whale-watchers, Arctic sun lovers and television crews. But, as yet, Michelin has resisted the urge to publish a Greenland gastronomic guide. It appears that most of its food is imported from Canada, although in the south excellent sheep are bred on cultivated salt grassland. Sheep, along with prawns and halibut, are the main food resources, except for – of course – musk ox, kittiwakes, seal, whale and reindeer.

Left: Barren or what?

Right: Spring is round this corner, winter is round the next

Overleaf: Glacier: a force of nature that creates icebergs and terrifies sailors; to a cook it could be a magnificent meringue

Left: Disko Island is not a nightclub

Right: We boarded the elegant *MV Disko* here at Ilulissat

It was ten o'clock at night and the *MV Disko* was steaming sedately past the massive pink- and azure-tinted Arctic meringues that, squinted at through this midnight sun, can resemble massive sculptured heads, cathedrals, swans, ghostly vessels or wedding cakes for the gods. I was sitting on the stern deck and, above the whoosh of the stern wave and the hum of the engines, I could hear the tiny explosions from the million-year-old chunk of iceberg on the stern of the ship.

The brightly painted

buildings of Greenland

Left: A breathtaking,
natural archway of ice

Right: Another fishy day
in paradise

The next morning, we bade farewell to the discreet luxury of the *Disko* and transferred on to a small fishing boat heading for the ice-floe-strewn fjord. There Inuit fishermen in tiny boats dodge the speeding floes as they fish for halibut with hand-lines. At this time of the year the fish have moved well north and the fishermen have moved with them. By night they camp on the inhospitable shores and each day they load their catch into a larger vessel that takes it down to the capital, Nuuk, for processing the next morning. The fishermen themselves will probably not eat the fish, but rather chew on pieces of dried whale or an occasional fresh seal stew.

Left: Iceberg!

Above right:

Inuit burial ground

Below right: Desolation

Overleaf: After the iron rush

After a couple of hours of filming, we set off in our little boat to our overnight accommodation, a journey of some two hours, so they said. But after a couple of the props got smashed, the half-night fell and the ice thickened, it took us eight hours to reach our desolate destination, a wooden bunk-house attached to a rock in the middle of absolutely nowhere. There was no jetty and we had to clamber up the precipitous rocks carrying all our equipment, to spend two sleepless hours in a mosquito-infested hell with no electricity, no running water and no sanitation, before continuing on our journey south. Although we had not eaten for some ten hours, none of us could face the seal blubber and potato stew offered us for breakfast by the warden of this place, which in fact turned out to be a sort of youth hostel-cum-trekking lodge and where, unbelievably, perfectly sane-looking people paid money to spend their summer holiday. But, hand on heart, I wouldn't have missed the experience for the world.

Our little boat sped past the now diminishing ice floes heading for Ilulissat and our first night in a hotel and civilization for some days. Hooray! We would wash, bathe, eat hot food, drink and phone home – little luxuries we had sorely missed. Ilulissat is a scruffy little settlement with brightly painted prefabricated buildings, gravel tracks, tethered huskies and a very busy fish harbour, but to us it seemed like paradise; when you travel as I do, paradise

Making hay while the sun shines, because it's back to work at the first sign of snow

'Ilulissat: it came up tails and it rhymed with whales so I headed back to the ship.'
Apologies to Captain Ahab and Bob Dylan

is a very fleeting state of mind. On the next day, it was decided, I would cook
on a large iceberg, conveniently parked a hundred metres from the hotel —
indeed it was right under our window. I was going to prepare two simple
dishes, one seared red fish soup, the other slivers of marinated, raw,
Greenland halibut. Both very simple. For the soup you need some good
chicken consommé or chicken stock, small fillets of red fish, snapper or
mullet, and a heaped tablespoon per person of a mixture of very finely
chopped carrot, onion, garlic, ginger, leeks, chilli, red and green pepper, and
celery. I also decided to add some marble-sized dumplings but you could use
a couple of Chinese wontons or vegetable ravioli which you can buy in the
supermarket. All you do is sear, on both sides, the little pieces of fish in a hot,
dry pan, poach the wonton, ravioli or dumplings in the chicken stock, put it
in bowls, float the seared fish on top and sprinkle on some of the raw, finely
chopped vegetables.

The halibut was even simpler. I cut thin slices of the raw fish, rather
like smoked salmon, squeezed fresh lemon juice over it, added a little olive
oil, sprinkled over some coarse sea salt along with some very finely chopped
chilli and refrigerated it — that is to say, left it on a rock for a while! I then
served it with warm croûtons fried in olive oil, crème fraîche mixed with finely
chopped beetroot and halves of hard-boiled egg topped with a little
mayonnaise and caviar and salmon eggs.

Right: Hopefully, the fine flavour of these Greenlandic
halibut justifies their cost. The work involved
in catching them is cold, dangerous and very hard

Far right: Even under the most adverse conditions, my
Spanish plancha never let me down

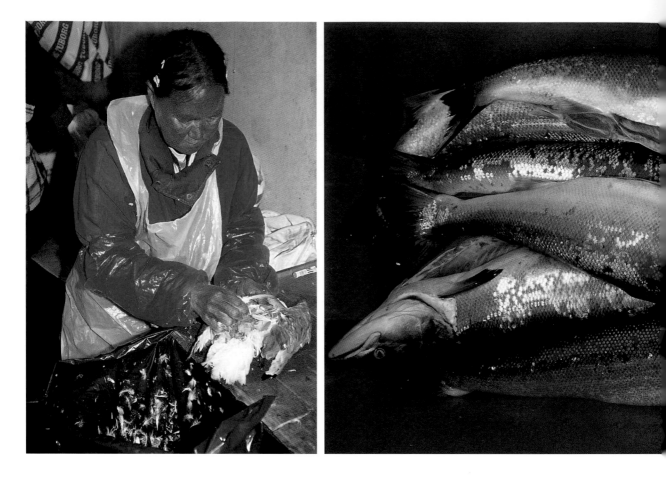

Anyway, back to the impending iceberg sketch. We were assured by an icebergologist that as long as we wore survival suits, everything would be OK. To my chagrin and dismay, when I awoke the next morning the iceberg had vamoosed – gone and sailed off into the sunset. When I say to my chagrin, I am, of course, lying. I was absolutely delighted that the blasted thing had gone; now all we had to do was clamber on to a tiny rock island in the harbour in the howling wind, do the cooking sketch and press on to the capital of Greenland, Nuuk (pop. 13,000) where I had no choice, if I was to acknowledge what Greenland was all about, but to cook whale and seal, which would undoubtedly infuriate and anger the well-intentioned but ill-informed. Just as the Australian Aboriginals, the indigenous people of that land, were nomadic hunter-gatherers for forty thousand years, so, for a similar period, the Greenland Inuit have been seal and whale hunters. These mammals provided

food, fur for clothing, fats and oils for heating and lighting, skins for making kayaks, bone for making tools, implements and jewellery and, very importantly, trade for the necessary things that Greenland itself could not provide.

Until I went to the market at Nuuk, all I knew about seals was that they were cute little things that sat on rocks, swam about occasionally and looked jolly nice. But when I saw one being butchered, I understood why they are so very important to the people of Greenland. Everything, every edible part of a domestic European pig is found in a seal, from the chitterlings (intestinal tubes) to the liver, lights, kidneys, bacon (aka blubber) loin and spare ribs. It is all there, just the same. And as pigskin is used for handbags, shoes et al., so is sealskin. So, to the delight of the local population, who, along with Greenland's press, TV and radio, had gathered to watch me cook

some whale and seal, I put on my sealskin hat, threw caution, morals and principles to the wind, an aquavit down my throat and committed what many will see as a crime against nature. I make no apologies; as they say, 'When in Rome . . .' and besides, I hadn't come all this way to cook hamburgers. So I cut some loin of seal into 1½ inch long strips, seared it in hot oil with finely chopped onions, garlic, ginger and chillies, stirred in some mild curry powder and cooked the lot together for a couple of minutes. I added some tomato purée and some coconut milk and simmered it for about ten minutes; then I put in some slivers of fresh coconut and served it in the coconut shell, garnished with fresh herbs and some very crisply fried onions.

I cooked the whale on the plancha. First I griddled pieces of spring onion, slivers of red and green pepper, strips of carrot, chopped chillies, garlic and ginger, snow peas, chunks of fresh pineapple and pieces of tomato, seared them quickly, mixed them together and seasoned them with salt and pepper. These I placed into a scooped-out half pineapple; then I quickly seared wafer-thin slices of whale on the plancha and popped them on top of the vegetables with a dash of soy sauce. Tra-la!

The next morning I carefully packed the hand-carved, soapstone whales' tails I had purchased into the 'Save the Whalers' T-shirt I had given me and took off in Greenlandair's trusty Dash 7 four-engined flying bus for the precious pastures of southern Greenland.

The community of Igaliku was first settled in the twelfth century by Eric the Red, an Icelandic entrepreneur and explorer who gave Greenland its name in order to encourage people from Iceland and the surrounding areas to settle there. He must have been one of the world's first estate agents, practised in the art of unprovable deception. About fifty people live in this community on the grassy slopes that run down to the beautiful fjord full of trout, salmon and other fish.

Across the fjord the mountains rose and the ice-cap glinted in the high, bright sun. For Greenland it was a very warm day and the whole village turned out to help, to watch, to feast and enjoy. Their nearest 'town' is three hours away by boat and the helicopter comes once or twice a month to bring

Spring in Igaliku

Greenlandic lamb is delicious, and I was particularly proud of this stuffed leg of lamb that I cooked in an excavated earth oven

supplies, ordered from a catalogue that offers everything from snow scooters, husky harnesses and hunting rifles to underwear, ice drills for fishing, kayaks and guitars. They provided me with a whole lamb to cook. They welded me a spit and cut me sheets of steel and provided bricks so that I could make an earth oven. This was real camp-fire cooking. I stuffed a boned-out shoulder of lamb with breadcrumbs mixed with water and egg, to which I added finely sliced onion, diced dried apricots, diced dried prunes, flaked almonds, parsley, garlic, mint and a dash of olive oil. I rolled it up, tied it with wire and popped it into my earth oven. Meanwhile, I diced the trimmings from the lamb, fried some thin slices of aubergine, sautéed some thin onion rings and made a béchamel sauce with some lamb stock. I sliced some raw potatoes into very thin discs and chopped up a couple of tomatoes. I fried the meat with garlic and rosemary, and stirred in the chopped tomato. Into a roasting dish I put a layer of onions, a layer of chopped meat, a layer of the fried aubergines, another layer of meat, more aubergines and onions, another layer of meat and then a layer of sliced potatoes, covered it with the béchamel and popped it into my earth oven next to the stuffed lamb. The remainder of the lamb, virtually the whole carcass, was sizzling gently on a spit over a wood fire.

While all that was cooking in the uncharted temperatures of earth ovens and wood fires, I sautéed finger-sized strips of musk ox with finely sliced onions and mushrooms in butter on my trusty portable gas stove. Once they were sealed I flamed them in aquavit, stirred in some sweet, hot paprika, stir-fried that till the paprika was well absorbed, added a tablespoon of tomato purée and poured in some sour cream; I served the finished dish with finely chopped pickled beetroot and pickled cucumber relish.

For the rest of the day, the villagers provided horses, food and beds. If they thought we were mad, daft or impractical city slickers hopelessly out of our depth in the wilderness, they did not show it. They, in common with everyone that we met in Greenland, could not do enough to help us and sincerely welcomed us to Greenland, their 'Greenland, the Beautiful Country' – which it is.

Index

A

aïoli: Fillets of Fish a la Plancha with Anchovy Aïoli, 123

almonds
Chicken with Almonds and Honey, 168
Couscous with Fish and Coconut Sauce, 113–14
Pilau Rice with Lamb or Goat, 99–100
Salmon a la Plancha, 110–11

anchovies
Braised Leg of Lamb with Turmeric, Capers, Anchovy and Red Peppers, 29
Fillets of Fish a la Plancha with Anchovy Aïoli, 123

apples
Fruit-alcohol-marinated Salmon with Apple and Chives, 126
Smoked Herring with Leek and Potato Cakes, 76

apricots (dried): Salmon a la Plancha, 110–11

aquavit
Bear with Lingonberries on a Celeriac Rosti, 58
Carbonade of Moose, 80–81
Eels Stewed in Red Wine, 134
Fresh Fruits with an Aquavit-glazed Sabayon, 62
Freshwater Swedish Crayfish Boiled Louisiana-style, 159
Fruit-alcohol-marinated Salmon with Apple and Chives, 126
Karasjok Reindeer Heart, 54
Sauté of Reindeer with Paprika, 55

asparagus: Poached Halibut with Steamed Vegetables and Green Pea Sauce, 142-3

Aylesbury duckling: Bortsch, 60

B

bacon
Chicken with Shiitake Mushrooms, 74
Eels Stewed in Red Wine, 134
Karasjok Reindeer Heart, 54
Sauté of Reindeer with Paprika, 55

Barbecued or Deep-fried Chicken with Lemon Sauce, 120, 122

bass: Grilled Char with an Asian Sweet and Sour Stir-fry, 52

beans see black beans; green beans

Bear with Lingonberries on a Celeriac Rosti, 58

beef
Bear with Lingonberries on a Celeriac Rosti, 58
Carbonade of Moose, 80–81
Floyd's Hamburger with Spiced Onion Relish, 184–5
Sauté of Reindeer with Paprika, 55
Swedish Hash, 183

beer: Carbonade of Moose, 80–81

beetroot
Bortsch, 60
Greenland halibut, 208
Halibut with Red Pepper Sauce and Beetroot Crisps, 40
Smoked Herring with Leek and Potato Cakes, 76

black beans: Steamed Bream with Black Bean Sauce, 177

black cherries: Smoked Loin of Pork in Black-cherry Sauce, 146

Bortsch, 60

Braised Ham with Root Vegetables and Pea-green Sauce, 124

Braised Leg of Lamb with Turmeric, Capers, Anchovy and Red Peppers, 29

brandy
Bear with Lingonberries on a Celeriac Rosti, 58
Chicken with Shiitake Mushrooms, 74
Crayfish Bisque, 64
Karasjok Reindeer Heart, 54
Sauté of Reindeer with Paprika, 55
Smoked Loin of Pork in Black-cherry Sauce, 146

bread
Fillets of Fish a la Plancha with Anchovy Aïoli, 123
Floyd's Real Taramasalata, 22
Stavanger Lobster and Fish Stew, 108–9

bream
Grilled Char with an Asian Sweet and Sour Stir-fry, 52
Stavanger Lobster and Fish Stew, 108–9
Steamed Bream with Black Bean Sauce, 177

C

Cajun seasoning: Freshwater Swedish Crayfish Boiled Louisiana-style, 159

capelin roe: Norwegian Potato Waffle with Caviars and Soured Cream, 116

capers
Braised Leg of Lamb with Turmeric, Capers, Anchovy and Red Peppers, 29
Salmon a la Plancha, 110–11

Carbonade of Moose, 80–81

carrots
Bortsch, 60
Braised Ham with Root Vegetables and Pea-green Sauce, 124
Braised Leg of Lamb with Turmeric, Capers, Anchovy and Red Peppers, 29
Carbonade of Moose, 80–81
Crayfish Bisque, 64

Emanuel Augustin's Swedish Summer Soup, 186

Fjord Fish Cakes with a Sweet and Sour Sauce, 43

Gratin of King Crab and Lettuce Parcels, 56–7

Lamb and Chick-pea Soup, 118

Poached Cod with Fresh Parsley Sauce, 23

Poached Halibut with Steamed Vegetables and Green Pea Sauce, 142-3

Poached Herring Fillets with Dill and Parsley Sauce, 115

seared red fish soup, 208

Stavanger Lobster and Fish Stew, 108–9

Steamed Bream with Black Bean Sauce, 177

cashew nuts: Pilau Rice with Lamb or Goat, 99–100

cauliflower: Emanuel Augustin's Swedish Summer Soup, 186

caviar
Greenland halibut, 208
Norwegian Potato Waffle with Caviars and Soured Cream, 116
Tartare of Char with Rosti Potato, 50

celeriac
Bear with Lingonberries on a Celeriac Rosti, 58
Warm Smoked Eel Salad with Chilled Parsley Sauce and Scrambled Eggs, 136

celery
Braised Leg of Lamb with Turmeric, Capers, Anchovy and Red Peppers, 29
Crayfish Bisque, 64
Gratin of King Crab and Lettuce Parcels, 56–7
Poached Cod with Fresh Parsley Sauce, 23
Poached Halibut with Steamed Vegetables and Green Pea Sauce, 142-3
seared red fish soup, 208
Stavanger Lobster and Fish Stew, 108–9

char
Grilled Char with an Asian Sweet and Sour Stir-fry, 52
Tartare of Char with Rosti Potato, 50

cheese: Gratin of King Crab and Lettuce Parcels, 56–7

cherries: Smoked Loin of Pork in Black-cherry Sauce, 146

cherry brandy: Smoked Loin of Pork in Black-cherry Sauce, 146

Cherry Heering liqueur: Smoked Loin of
    Pork in Black-cherry Sauce, 146
chick-peas: Lamb and Chick-pea Soup,
    118
chicken
    Barbecued or Deep-fried Chicken with
        Lemon Sauce, 120, 122
    Chicken with Almonds and Honey, 168
    Chicken with Shiitake Mushrooms, 74
chillies
    Couscous with Fish and Coconut
        Sauce, 113–4
    Floyd's Freshwater Fish Fiesta, 174
    Greenland halibut, 208
    Grilled Char with an Asian Sweet and
        Sour Stir-fry, 52
    Medallions of White Fish or
        Scallops, 46
    Noodle and Shellfish Soup, 181
    Pilau Rice with Lamb or Goat, 99–100
    Salt Cod with Potatoes in Tomato
        Sauce, 48
    seared red fish soup, 208
    Steamed Bream with Black Bean
        Sauce, 177
    Tartare of Char with Rosti Potato, 50
Chinese black beans: Steamed Bream
    with Black Bean Sauce, 177
chives: Fruit-alcohol-marinated Salmon
    with Apple and Chives, 126
cider: Braised Ham with Root Vegetables
    and Pea-green Sauce, 124
clams: Rice with Rabbit and Shellfish,
    188
coconut milk
    Couscous with Fish and Coconut
        Sauce, 113–14
    Noodle and Shellfish Soup, 181
cod
    Fillets of Fish a la Plancha with
        Anchovy Aïoli, 123
    Fjord Fish Cakes with a Sweet and
        Sour Sauce, 43
    Floyd's Real Taramasalata, 22
    Medallions of White Fish or Scallops,
        46
    Poached Cod with Fresh Parsley Sauce,
        23
    Salt Cod with Potatoes in Tomato
        Sauce, 48
cognac
    Eels Stewed in Red Wine, 134
    Karasjok Reindeer Heart, 54
    Sauté of Reindeer with Paprika, 55
corn on the cob: Freshwater Swedish
    Crayfish Boiled Louisiana-style, 159
courgettes
    Iced Lemon Courgettes, 189
    Lamb and Chick-pea Soup, 118
couscous
    Couscous with Fish and Coconut
        Sauce, 113–14
    Couscous with Shellfish, 114

crab
    Crayfish Bisque, 64
    Gratin of King Crab and Lettuce
        Parcels, 56–7
crayfish
    Crayfish Bisque, 64
    Freshwater Swedish Crayfish Boiled
        Louisiana-style, 159
    Noodle and Shellfish Soup, 181
    Stavanger Lobster and Fish Stew,
        108–9
cream
    Fresh Herring Fillets with a Lemon
        and Mustard Cream, 78
    Mussels in Saffron Cream, 90
    Norwegian Potato Waffle with Caviars
        and Soured Cream, 116
crème de cassis
    Bear with Lingonberries on a Celeriac
        Rosti, 58
    Fruit-alcohol-marinated Salmon with
        Apple and Chives, 126
crème fraîche
    Greenland halibut, 208
    Halibut with Red Pepper Sauce and
        Beetroot Crisps, 40
    Smoked Herring with Leek and Potato
        Cakes, 76
    Tartare of Char with Rosti Potato, 50
croûtons: Greenland halibut, 208
crowberry wine: Karasjok Reindeer
    Heart, 54
crystallized fruit: Pilau Rice with Lamb
    or Goat, 99–100
cucumbers
    Grilled Char with an Asian Sweet and
        Sour Stir-fry, 52
    Salmon a la Plancha, 110–11
    Tandoori Perch, 175
currants: Couscous with Fish and
    Coconut Sauce, 113–14

D

dill: Poached Herring Fillets with Dill
    and Parsley Sauce, 115
dill cucumber: Salmon a la Plancha,
    110–11
duckling: Bortsch, 60
dumplings: seared red fish soup, 208

E

eels
    Eels Stewed in Red Wine, 134
    Warm Smoked Eel Salad with Chilled
        Parsley Sauce and Scrambled Eggs,
        136
eggs
    Braised Leg of Lamb with Turmeric,
        Capers, Anchovy and Red Peppers,
        29
    Fresh Fruits with an Aquavit-glazed
        Sabayon, 62
    Greenland halibut, 204

Norwegian Potato Waffle with Caviars
    and Soured Cream, 116
Stavanger Lobster and Fish Stew,
    108–9
Warm Smoked Eel Salad with Chilled
    Parsley Sauce and Scrambled Eggs,
    136
Emanuel Augustin's Swedish Summer
    Soup, 186

F

fennel: Poached Halibut with Steamed
    Vegetables and Green Pea Sauce,
    142-3
fish
    Fillets of Fish a la Plancha with
        Anchovy Aïoli, 123
    Medallions of White Fish or Scallops,
        46
    see also individual fish
Fjord Fish Cakes with a Sweet and Sour
    Sauce, 43
Floyd's Freshwater Fish Fiesta, 174
Floyd's Hamburger with Spiced Onion
    Relish, 184–5
Floyd's Real Taramasalata, 22
Fresh Fruits with an Aquavit-glazed
    Sabayon, 62
Fresh Herring Fillets with a Lemon and
    Mustard Cream, 78
Fresh Tomato Sauce, 49
Freshwater Swedish Crayfish Boiled
    Louisiana-style, 159
fruit
    Fresh Fruits with an Aquavit-glazed
        Sabayon, 62
    see also individual fruits
Fruit-alcohol-marinated Salmon with
    Apple and Chives, 126

G

gammon: Braised Ham with Root
    Vegetables and Pea-green Sauce, 124
garlic mayonnaise: Stavanger Lobster and
    Fish Stew, 108–9
gin: Carbonade of Moose, 80–1
ginger (lime and ginger marinade):
    Tartare of Char with Rosti Potato, 50
goat
    Pilau Rice with Lamb or Goat, 99–100
    Pilau Rice with Lamb or Goat Kebabs
        with Saffron Yoghurt, 101
Gratin of King Crab and Lettuce Parcels,
    56-7
green beans
    Emanuel Augustin's Swedish Summer
        Soup, 186
    Poached Halibut with Steamed
        Vegetables and Green Pea Sauce,
        142-3
green peppers
    seared red fish soup, 204

Steamed Bream with Black Bean
Sauce, 177
Whole Herring Cooked in a
Mediterranean Vinaigrette, 79
Grilled Char with an Asian Sweet and
Sour Stir-fry, 52

H

haddock
Fillets of Fish a la Plancha with
Anchovy Aïoli, 123
Fjord Fish Cakes with a Sweet and
Sour Sauce, 43
Stavanger Lobster and Fish Stew,
108–9
hake: Stavanger Lobster and Fish Stew,
108–9
halibut
Fillets of Fish a la Plancha with
Anchovy Aïoli, 123
Greenland halibut, 208
Halibut with Red Pepper Sauce
and Beetroot Crisps, 40
Poached Halibut with Horseradish,
176
Poached Halibut with Steamed
Vegetables and Green Pea Sauce,
142-3
ham: Braised Ham with Root Vegetables
and Pea-green Sauce, 124
hamburgers: Floyd's Hamburger with
Spiced Onion Relish, 184–5
harissa: Stavanger Lobster and Fish Stew,
108–9
hash: Swedish Hash, 183
herbs (herb salsa): Salmon a la Plancha,
110–11
herring
Fresh Herring Fillets with a Lemon
and Mustard Cream, 78
Poached Herring Fillets with Dill and
Parsley Sauce, 115
Smoked Herring with Leek and Potato
Cakes, 76
Whole Herring Cooked in a
Mediterranean Vinaigrette, 79
honey: Chicken with Almonds and Honey,
168
horseradish
Poached Halibut with Horseradish,
176
Poached Halibut with Steamed
Vegetables and Green Pea Sauce,
142-3

I

Iced Lemon Courgettes, 189

J

Japanese tempura batter: Barbecued or
Deep-fried Chicken with Lemon Sauce,
120, 122
juniper berries

Bortsch, 60
Carbonade of Moose, 80–1
Sauté of Reindeer with Paprika, 55

K

Karasjok Reindeer Heart, 54
kebabs: Pilau Rice with Lamb or Goat
Kebabs with Saffron Yoghurt, 101

L

lager
Carbonade of Moose, 80–1
Freshwater Swedish Crayfish Boiled
Louisiana-style, 159
Warm Smoked Eel Salad with Chilled
Parsley Sauce and Scrambled Eggs,
136
lamb
Braised Leg of Lamb with Turmeric,
Capers, Anchovy and Red Peppers,
29
Karasjok Reindeer Heart, 54
Lamb and Chick-pea Soup, 118
Pilau Rice with Lamb or Goat, 99–100
Pilau Rice with Lamb or Goat Kebabs
with Saffron Yoghurt, 101
langoustines: Rice with Rabbit and
Shellfish, 188
leeks
Bortsch, 60
Braised Leg of Lamb with Turmeric,
Capers, Anchovy and Red Peppers,
29
Emanuel Augustin's Swedish Summer
Soup, 186
seared red fish soup, 208
Smoked Herring with Leek and Potato
Cakes, 76
Stavanger Lobster and Fish Stew, 108–9
lemons
Barbecued or Deep-fried Chicken with
Lemon Sauce, 120, 122
Floyd's Real Taramasalata, 22
Fresh Herring Fillets with a Lemon
and Mustard Cream, 78
Freshwater Swedish Crayfish Boiled
Louisiana-style, 159
Iced Lemon Courgettes, 189
Lemon Pepper Perch, 178
lettuce: Gratin of King Crab and Lettuce
Parcels, 56–7
limes (lime and ginger marinade): Tartare
of Char with Rosti Potato, 50
lingonberries: Bear with Lingonberries on
a Celeriac Rosti, 58
lobster
Crayfish Bisque, 64
Stavanger Lobster and Fish Stew,
108–9
lumpfish roe
Norwegian Potato Waffle with Caviars
and Soured Cream, 116
Tartare of Char with Rosti Potato, 50

M

mackerel
Couscous with Fish and Coconut
Sauce, 113–14
Tartare of Char with Rosti Potato, 50
madeira: Karasjok Reindeer Heart, 54
mangetout
Emanuel Augustin's Swedish Summer
soup, 186
Poached Halibut with Steamed
Vegetables and Green Pea Sauce,
142-3
marinade (lime and ginger): Tartare of
Char with Rosti Potato, 50
mayonnaise
Greenland halibut, 208
Lemon Pepper Perch, 178
Salmon a la Plancha, 110–11
Stavanger Lobster and Fish Stew,
108–9
Medallions of White Fish or Scallops, 46
milk
Emanuel Augustin's Swedish Summer
Soup, 186
Poached Cod with Fresh Parsley
Sauce, 23
monkfish: Medallions of White Fish or
Scallops, 46
moose: Carbonade of Moose, 80–81
mushrooms
Chicken with Shiitake Mushrooms, 74
Eels Stewed in Red Wine, 134
Karasjok Reindeer Heart, 54
mussels
Couscous with Shellfish, 114
Mussels in Saffron Cream, 90
Rice with Rabbit and Shellfish, 188
mustard: Fresh Herring Fillets with a
Lemon and Mustard Cream, 78

N

Noodle and Shellfish Soup, 181
Norwegian Potato Waffle with Caviars and
Soured Cream, 116

O

Okra Soup, 180
onions
Bortsch, 60
Braised Ham with Root Vegetables and
Pea-green Sauce, 124
Braised Leg of Lamb with Turmeric,
Capers, Anchovy and Red Peppers,
29
Carbonade of Moose, 80–81
Chicken with Almonds and Honey, 168
Chicken with Shiitake Mushrooms, 74
Couscous with Fish and Coconut
Sauce, 113–14
Eels Stewed in Red Wine, 134
Emanuel Augustin's Swedish Summer
Soup, 186
Floyd's Freshwater Fish Fiesta, 174

Floyd's Hamburger with Spiced Onion
  Relish, 184–5
Gratin of King Crab and Lettuce
  Parcels, 56–7
Iced Lemon Courgettes, 189
Karasjok Reindeer Heart, 54
Lamb and Chick-pea Soup, 118
Medallions of White Fish or Scallops,
  46
Mussels in Saffron Cream, 90
Okra Soup, 180
Pilau Rice with Lamb or Goat, 99–100
Poached Cod with Fresh Parsley Sauce,
  23
Rice with Rabbit and Shellfish, 188
Salt Cod with Potatoes in Tomato
  Sauce, 48
Sauté of Reindeer with Paprika, 55
seared red fish soup, 208
Stavanger Lobster and Fish Stew,
  108–9
Swedish Hash, 183
Tartare of Char with Rosti Potato, 50
see also red onions
oranges: Freshwater Swedish Crayfish
  Boiled Louisiana-style, 159

P

paprika: Sauté of Reindeer with Paprika,
  55
parsley
  Poached Cod with Fresh Parsley Sauce,
    23
  Poached Herring Fillets with Dill and
    Parsley Sauce, 115
  Warm Smoked Eel Salad with Chilled
    Parsley Sauce and Scrambled Eggs,
    136
peanuts: Pilau Rice with Lamb or Goat,
  99–100
peas
  Rice with Rabbit and Shellfish, 188
  see also mangetout; petits pois
peppers *see* green peppers; red peppers
perch
  Lemon Pepper Perch, 178
  Tandoori Perch, 175
petits pois
  Braised Ham with Root Vegetables and
    Pea-green Sauce, 124
  Poached Halibut with Steamed
    Vegetables and Green Pea Sauce,
    142-3
pike: Floyd's Freshwater Fish Fiesta, 174
Pilau Rice with Lamb or Goat, 99–100
Pilau Rice with Lamb or Goat Kebabs
  with Saffron Yoghurt, 101
pine kernels
  Pilau Rice with Lamb or Goat, 99–100
  Salmon a la Plancha, 110–11
pineapple: Grilled Char with an Asian
  Sweet and Sour Stir-fry, 52
plovers' eggs: Norwegian Potato Waffle

with Caviars and Soured Cream, 116
Poached Cod with Fresh Parsley Sauce,
  23
Poached Halibut with Horseradish, 176
Poached Halibut with Steamed Vegetables
  and Green Pea Sauce, 142–3
Poached Herring Fillets with Dill and
  Parsley Sauce, 115
polenta: Fjord Fish Cakes with a Sweet
  and Sour Sauce, 43
pork
  Bear with Lingonberries on a Celeriac
    Rosti, 58
  Smoked Loin of Pork in Black-cherry
    Sauce, 146
port: Karasjok Reindeer Heart, 54
potato flour: Fjord Fish Cakes with a
  Sweet and Sour Sauce, 43
potatoes
  Bear with Lingonberries on a Celeriac
    Rosti, 58
  Braised Ham with Root Vegetables and
    Pea-green Sauce, 124
  Freshwater Swedish Crayfish Boiled
    Louisiana-style, 159
  Norwegian Potato Waffle with Caviars
    and Soured Cream, 116
  Poached Halibut with Horseradish,
    176
  Salmon a la Plancha, 110–11
  Salt Cod with Potatoes in Tomato
    Sauce, 48
  Smoked Herring with Leek and Potato
    Cakes, 76
  Stavanger Lobster and Fish Stew,
    108–9
  Swedish Hash, 183
  Tartare of Char with Rosti Potato, 50
poussin: Barbecued or Deep-fried
  Chicken with Lemon Sauce, 120, 122
prawns
  Noodle and Shellfish Soup, 181
  Rice with Rabbit and Shellfish, 188
prunes: Salmon a la Plancha, 110–11

Q

quails' eggs: Norwegian Potato Waffle
  with Caviars and Soured Cream, 116

R

rabbit: Rice with Rabbit and Shellfish,
  188
raisins
  Couscous with Fish and Coconut
    Sauce, 113–14
  Floyd's Hamburger with Spiced Onion
    Relish, 184–5
  Pilau Rice with Lamb or Goat, 99–100
ravioli, vegetable: seared red fish soup,
  208
red mullet
  Couscous with Fish and Coconut
    Sauce, 113–14

seared red fish soup, 208
Stavanger Lobster and Fish Stew,
  108–9
red onions
  Fresh Tomato Sauce, 49
  Freshwater Swedish Crayfish Boiled
    Louisiana-style, 159
  Norwegian Potato Waffle with Caviars
    and Soured Cream, 116
  Salmon a la Plancha, 110–11
  Whole Herring Cooked in a
    Mediterranean Vinaigrette, 79
red peppers
  Braised Leg of Lamb with Turmeric,
    Capers, Anchovy and Red Peppers,
    29
  Couscous with Fish and Coconut
    Sauce, 113–14
  Fjord Fish Cakes with a Sweet and
    Sour Sauce, 43
  Floyd's Freshwater Fish Fiesta, 174
  Grilled Char with an Asian Sweet and
    Sour Stir-fry, 52
  Halibut with Red Pepper Sauce and
    Beetroot Crisps, 40
  Rice with Rabbit and Shellfish, 188
  seared red fish soup, 208
  Steamed Bream with Black Bean
    Sauce, 177
  Whole Herring Cooked in a
    Mediterranean Vinaigrette, 79
red snapper
  Stavanger Lobster and Fish Stew,
    108–9
  seared red fish soup, 208
red wine
  Chicken with Shiitake Mushrooms, 74
  Eels Stewed in Red Wine, 134
redcurrant compote: Bear with
  Lingonberries on a Celeriac Rosti, 58
reindeer
  Karasjok Reindeer Heart, 54
  Sauté of Reindeer with Paprika, 55
relishes
  Floyd's Freshwater Fish Fiesta, 174
  Floyd's Hamburger with Spiced Onion
    Relish, 184–5
  Lemon Pepper Perch, 178
  Tandoori Perch, 175
rice
  Pilau Rice with Lamb or Goat, 99–100
  Pilau Rice with Lamb or Goat Kebabs
    with Saffron Yoghurt, 101
  Rice with Rabbit and Shellfish, 188
  Salmon a la Plancha, 110–11
rice noodles: Noodle and Shellfish Soup,
  181
rice wine: Grilled Char with an Asian
  Sweet and Sour Stir-fry, 52
rostis
  Bear with Lingonberries on a Celeriac
    Rosti, 58
  Tartare of Char with Rosti Potato, 50

S

sabayon: Fresh Fruits with an Aquavit-glazed Sabayon, 62

saffron
Mussels in Saffron Cream, 90
Pilau Rice with Lamb or Goat Kebabs with Saffron Yoghurt, 101

salads
Fruit-alcohol-marinated Salmon with Apple and Chives, 126
Warm Smoked Eel Salad with Chilled Parsley Sauce and Scrambled Eggs, 136

salmon
Fruit-alcohol-marinated Salmon with Apple and Chives, 126
Salmon a la Plancha, 110–11
Tartare of Char with Rosti Potato, 50

salsa (herb salsa): Salmon a la Plancha, 110–11

Salt Cod with Potatoes in Tomato Sauce, 48

sauces
Barbecued or Deep-fried Chicken with Lemon Sauce, 120, 122
Braised Ham with Root Vegetables and Pea-green Sauce, 124
Sauté of Reindeer with Paprika, 55
Couscous with Fish and Coconut Sauce, 113–14
Fjord Fish Cakes with a Sweet and Sour Sauce, 43
Fresh Tomato Sauce, 49
Halibut with Red Pepper Sauce and Beetroot Crisps, 40
Medallions of White Fish or Scallops, 46
Poached Cod with Fresh Parsley Sauce, 23
Poached Halibut with Steamed Vegetables and Green Pea Sauce, 142–3
Poached Herring Fillets with Dill and Parsley Sauce, 115
Salt Cod with Potatoes in Tomato Sauce, 48
Smoked Loin of Pork in Black-cherry Sauce, 146
Steamed Bream with Black Bean Sauce, 177
Warm Smoked Eel Salad with Chilled Parsley Sauce and Scrambled Eggs, 136

scallops
Couscous with Shellfish, 114
Medallions of White Fish or Scallops, 46
Noodle and Shellfish Soup, 181

seagulls' eggs
Braised Leg of Lamb with Turmeric, Capers, Anchovy and Red Peppers, 29

Norwegian Potato Waffle with Caviars and Soured Cream, 116

shallots
Chicken with Shiitake Mushrooms, 74
Eels Stewed in Red Wine, 134
Mussels in Saffron Cream, 90
Smoked Loin of Pork in Black-cherry Sauce, 146

sherry: Grilled Char with an Asian Sweet and Sour Stir-fry, 52

shiitake mushrooms: Chicken with Shiitake Mushrooms, 74

Smoked Herring with Leek and Potato Cakes, 76

Smoked Loin of Pork in Black-cherry Sauce, 146

soups
Bortsch, 60
Crayfish Bisque, 64
Emanuel Augustin's Swedish Summer Soup, 186
Lamb and Chick-pea Soup, 118
Noodle and Shellfish Soup, 181
Okra Soup, 180
seared red fish soup, 208

spring onions
Emanuel Augustin's Swedish Summer Soup, 186
Fjord Fish Cakes with a Sweet and Sour Sauce, 43
Grilled Char with an Asian Sweet and Sour Stir-fry, 52
Noodle and Shellfish Soup, 181
Poached Halibut with Steamed Vegetables and Green Pea Sauce, 142-3
Poached Herring Fillets with Dill and Parsley Sauce, 115
Steamed Bream with Black Bean Sauce, 177

Stavanger Lobster and Fish Stew, 108–9

Steamed Bream with Black Bean Sauce, 177

stews: Stavanger Lobster and Fish Stew, 108–9

stout: Carbonade of Moose, 80–81

sultanas
Couscous with Fish and Coconut Sauce, 113–14
Pilau Rice with Lamb or Goat, 99–100

Swedish Hash, 183

T

tamarind extract: Couscous with Fish and Coconut Sauce, 113–14

Tandoori Perch, 175

Tartare of Char with Rosti Potato, 50

tomatoes
Crayfish Bisque, 64
Fillets of Fish a la Plancha with Anchovy Aïoli, 123
Floyd's Freshwater Fish Fiesta, 174

Fresh Tomato Sauce, 49
Grilled Char with an Asian Sweet and Sour Stir-fry, 52
Okra Soup, 180
Sauté of Reindeer with Paprika, 55
Salmon a la Plancha, 110–11
Whole Herring Cooked in a Mediterranean Vinaigrette, 79

trout
Grilled Char with an Asian Sweet and Sour Stir-fry, 52
Tartare of Char with Rosti Potato, 50

turmeric: Braised Leg of Lamb with Turmeric, Capers, Anchovy and Red Peppers, 29

turnips: Braised Ham with Root Vegetables and Pea-green Sauce, 124

V

veal
Carbonade of Moose, 80–81
Sauté of Reindeer with Paprika, 55

venison
Bear with Lingonberries on a Celeriac Rosti, 58
Sauté of Reindeer with Paprika, 55

vinaigrette: Whole Herring Cooked in a Mediterranean Vinaigrette, 79

vodka
Barbecued or Deep-fried Chicken with Lemon Sauce, 120, 122
Fruit-alcohol-marinated Salmon with Apple and Chives, 126

W

waffles: Norwegian Potato Waffle with Caviars and Soured Cream, 116

Warm Smoked Eel Salad with Chilled Parsley Sauce and Scrambled Eggs, 136

white wine
Crayfish Bisque, 64
Fresh Fruits with an Aquavit-glazed Sabayon, 62
Gratin of King Crab and Lettuce Parcels, 56–7
Stavanger Lobster and Fish Stew, 108–9

Whole Herring Cooked in a Mediterranean Vinaigrette, 79

wine *see* crowberry wine; red wine; rice wine; white wine

wontons: seared red fish soup, 208

Y

yoghurt
Pilau Rice with Lamb or Goat Kebabs with Saffron Yoghurt, 101
Tandoori Perch, 175

Z

Zander with Piquant Sauce, 174